Ethics, Evil, and Fiction

COLIN McGINN

CLARENDON PRESS · OXFORD

OXFORD
UNIVERSITY PRESS

Great Clarendon Street, Oxford OX2 6DP

Oxford University Press is a department of the University of Oxford.
It furthers the University's objective of excellence in research, scholarship,
and education by publishing worldwide in

Oxford New York

Athens Auckland Bangkok Bogotá Buenos Aires Calcutta
Cape Town Chennai Dar es Salaam Delhi Florence Hong Kong Istanbul
Karachi Kuala Lumpur Madrid Melbourne Mexico City Mumbai
Nairobi Paris São Paulo Singapore Taipei Tokyo Toronto Warsaw

with associated companies in Berlin Ibadan

Oxford is a registered trade mark of Oxford University Press
in the UK and in certain other countries

Published in the United States
by Oxford University Press Inc., New York

British Library Cataloguing in Publication Data

Data available

Library of Congress Cataloging in Publication Data
McGinn, Colin, 1950–
Ethics, evil, and fiction / Colin McGinn.
Includes bibliographical references.
1. Ethics. 2. Ethics in literature. I. Title.
BJ46.M34 1997 170–dc21 97–4157

ISBN 0–19–823716–2
ISBN 0–19–823877–0 (Pbk.)

Printed in Great Britain
on acid-free paper by
Biddles Ltd
Guildford and King's Lynn

PREFACE

Probably the most pressing question about any area of philosophy is: how is it to be done? What is the right *method* to adopt in discovering something philosophically worthwhile? Here is where philosophical debate is apt to rage most fiercely. Many different methodological proposals have had their day: some have taken introspection to be the right method; some have favoured the methods of the physical sciences; some have seen mathematics as the appropriate basis; some have proposed a phenomenological approach, suspending the 'natural standpoint'; some have suggested that the analysis of language is the key; some have urged the merits of cognitive science. Most of the major revolutions in philosophy have been methodological, not theoretical—new ways of doing things, not new theories of things. No doubt this state of affairs carries a deep metaphilosophical lesson, which is perhaps not altogether sanguine. In any case, methodological anxiety is endemic to the subject.

Moral philosophy is no exception. Our aim is to shed light on aspects of life that involve moral notions (to put it as untendentiously as possible). Part of the problem here is knowing what to count as a moral notion; also what other notions need to be introduced in connection with moral notions. But, even once some decision has been made about these questions, there is still the question of what sort of method to adopt—of where, and how, to look for moral illumination. The tendency has been, naturally enough, to borrow whatever methodological assumptions have been made in other areas of philosophy, such as metaphysics and epistemology. This is not necessarily a sound procedure; it may well be that ethics calls for an approach that is distinctive to that subject-matter—that reflects its specific character. What we should certainly avoid is any preconceived method that *excludes* potentially fruitful avenues of reflection.

This book is written in the conviction that that is precisely what has happened with moral philosophy. In particular, the

potential contributions of literary fiction have been systematically neglected. For fiction fails to conform to any of the methodological paradigms that have dominated philosophy at large. Yet
in fiction we find ethical themes treated with a depth and resonance that is unmatched in human culture. Literature is where
moral thinking lives and breathes on the page. Philosophers of
morality therefore need to pay attention to it. And, if they do, it
is likely that the field of moral philosophy will take on a quite different complexion and shape.

My own route into this perspective came from two separate,
though connected, circumstances. The first was my own interest
in writing fiction. Having written two novels (one of them published: *The Space Trap*, Duckworth, 1992) and several short stories,
I became more actively aware of the way in which moral considerations enter intimately into the construction of fictional works.
The novelist must constantly treat of moral questions, and take
some position on them. The second circumstance was that I vol-
unteered to teach a course at Rutgers University that was otherwise about to go extinct. Called 'Philosophical Ideas in
Literature', this was a course in which the instructor could
choose whatever texts he or she liked and discuss them in any
way that seemed philosophically relevant. I chose some of my
favourite novels and tried to shape the course around that choice,
instead of settling on a philosophical theme and then finding
books (good or bad) that dealt with that theme in some way. The
first novel I taught was Nabokov's *Lolita*, chosen because of its
great distinction as a literary work and the emotional power of its
story. The philosophical theme that naturally emerged was good
and evil; and that was how the course acquired the shape it did.
Teaching this course was a very interesting (and demanding)
experience for me, because no recognized method existed by
which to pursue the kinds of issues I found in the works chosen.
Yet the moral material was as rich and dense as one could wish.
Nevertheless, the response of the students encouraged me to
think that this was a fruitful way to approach moral questions;
and the students in that class produced some of the best work
that I have ever seen.

Ideally, this way of doing moral philosophy is conducted by a
close reading of the literary text, with detailed comments on the
characters and scenes that are presented. I like to let the moral

issues develop naturally in step with the narrative. But this is not really feasible in a book such as this one, so here I have adopted a more selective and lofty approach, though still with a good deal of concrete detail. Much of what I have to say, however, has its origin in the close study of the relevant literary texts, the results emerging from the details of the story. The best way to read what I have written would be first to study the fictional texts themselves, preferably with someone else, discussing the details of what happens, and then turn to my discussion afterwards. I do not intend my discussions to be anything but adjuncts to the act of actually reading and assessing the works I am interpreting.

The earlier parts of the book are more orthodox in form, dealing with some standard questions in metaethics. Here I must confess that one of my motives in treating these topics is my repugnance for all kinds of relativism, scepticism, and subjectivism about morality. I have always found such views not only intellectually groundless but also morally appalling. My underlying aim is to show that it is possible, and necessary, to detach moral objectivity from any religious world-view—so that we do not need to believe in God in order to find morality both important and binding. The decline of religion is no reason to accept a decline in morality. What is wanted, then, is a philosophy of morality that shows it to be an area of truth and knowledge in good standing, despite the absence of the divine authority that has traditionally been supposed to give it substance. That is what I set out to do in the second and third chapters.

The book is rather mixed both in topic and level of difficulty. Since I want it to be read by the general reader and not just by professional philosophers, I have written the more abstract chapters with the minimum of scholarly apparatus, hoping that my professional colleagues will allow me a pinch of salt and add the curlicues necessary to achieve full analytical rigour. Still, I cannot pretend that these early chapters will be easy reading for anyone but the philosophically trained, at least in places. My advice for non-philosophical readers is to read over these chapters without trying to understand every detail of what is said: the general drift should come through, and the finer points are not essential to grasping the basic arguments. The level of difficulty lets up considerably in Chapter 4, at which point there will no longer be any reason to crease your forehead in exasperated perplexity.

I take the themes of this book very seriously and would like the reader to share my concerns. This has not prevented me, however, from adopting a lighter touch at various points, and I hope the reader will not think me flippant or irreverent. One of the great devices of serious fiction is humour, along with its playmates archness and irony; I have not suppressed these tendencies where they seemed appropriate.

I am grateful to quite a number of people for their comments and encouragement. Malcolm Budd and Thomas Nagel kindly read an early draft and made helpful comments. The students in my classes were a source of stimulation and amusement. Conversations with the following people were also appreciated: Noam Chomsky, Robert van Gulick, Anne Hollander, Elizabeth Hollander, Mark Johnston, Peter Kivy, Kathleen Mancini, Robert Matthews, Aaron Meskin, Jonathan Miller, Eileen O'Neil, Jed Perl, Consuelo Preti, Galen Strawson (I hope I haven't forgotten anybody). In connection with the material on evil, a couple of people (who will remain nameless) stimulated my thinking by way of example; it cannot be said that I am grateful to them for this.

My motto in this book is: when it comes to morality, there is more truth in fictional truth than is dreamt of by philosophers.

New York   *Colin McGinn*
May 1996

CONTENTS

Introduction: The Scope
of Moral Philosophy

What should be the domain of moral philosophy? With what sorts of question should it deal? There has always been some uncertainty about this question, with the field expanding or contracting according to the prevailing methodological assumptions and conception of the philosophical discipline. As practised in contemporary analytical philosophy, ethics is generally taken to have two departments—metaethics and normative ethics. Metaethics is the study of abstract metaphysical questions about the nature of ethical value; it asks whether ethical judgements are objective or subjective, absolute or relative, whether ethical statements are genuinely fact-stating, whether all moral value reduces to the maximization of utility, whether the authority of ethical requirements issues from a divine source, and so on. These are the more 'philosophical' questions that arise about moral value; and they regularly connect with other areas of philosophy in essential ways. Normative ethics, on the other hand, is taken to include practical questions in which ethical notions are essentially employed; it concerns itself with such issues as the morality of abortion, the conduct of war, the justifiability of censorship, euthanasia, animal rights, drunk driving, and so on. These questions are about what it is right to do in specific concrete circumstances.

Questions of normative ethics joined with questions of metaethics only recently in analytical philosophy. Once neglected, practical ethics has become recognized as a field in which philosophical expertise could yield rewards, and the addition of these questions has enriched the domain over which the moral philosopher might profitably roam. It has become accepted that a philosophical ethics confined purely to traditional metaethical questions is too narrow—that there is a range of ethical topics that is both philosophical in character and not comprehended by metaethics. And this enrichment has helped to stave off the charge, frequently made, that ethics, as practised by academic philosophers, is an arid and 'irrelevant' pursuit, in which the questions of greatest ethical importance are systematically neglected. More bluntly, there was—and still is—a feeling in some quarters that standard moral philosophy is a bore, failing to engage with what is really morally interesting. Normative ethics promises to inject some life and substance into the usual abstract aridities.

Now it is not that I agree with this dismissive attitude towards metaethics, though I do agree that there is room, and need, for normative ethics.[1] For much of the early and middle twentieth century the domain of moral philosophy was indeed conceived too narrowly. But I do not believe that the addition of practical ethics has sufficiently remedied the narrowness. There are still areas of moral interest that are not properly comprehended in the usual bipartite conception of the subject. So moral philosophy is still not living up to what we have a right to expect of it. And it is not merely that there are new subjects that need to be included; new methods and styles are necessary in order to incorporate the neglected questions. The aim of the moral philosopher is to do justice to the varieties of moral experience, to the entire range of ethical life, and this, I believe, requires us to go beyond the usual assumptions and methods. There is more to the moral life than what ethical words mean and what we should do about this and that.

In this book, one of my main concerns is to consider moral *character* from a philosophical point of view. This is by no means unheard of (Aristotle was onto it long ago),[2] but the way I want to approach the subject is perhaps somewhat unorthodox. I shall focus on the characters of certain fictional characters (the verbal coincidence is instructive) and this will inevitably involve me in questions of textual interpretation and exposition.[3] One purpose

[1] I have even written a book about it: *Moral Literacy*.

[2] Aristotle, *Nicomachean Ethics*.

[3] Martha Nussbaum, in *Love's Knowledge*, has also sought to connect moral philosophy with literature, though her approach is rather different from mine. See also Richard Rorty, *Contingency, Irony, and Solidarity*, Part III—which again differs from me both in style and substance.

of fiction is to present and reveal character in such a way as to invite moral appraisal: we are brought to enter into someone's character as it is expressed in feeling and action, and we react to this with various evaluative attitudes—affective as well as cognitive. And one purpose of literary criticism or commentary is (or ought to be) to make clear the ethical import of the actions and experiences of fictional characters. Thus questions of ethics intersect with artistic and literary questions. Given that works of literature offer a compelling route into questions of character ethics, we need, as philosophers, to develop ways of talking about the literary works themselves, and these ways may well not coincide with the ways appropriate to other kinds of literary study. In this book I shall discuss two fictional characters in some depth—Dorian Gray in Oscar Wilde's *The Picture of Dorian Gray* and the 'monster' in Mary Shelley's *Frankenstein*—with the hope of shedding light on them in their own right, and also to illustrate the kind of study that seems to me fruitful. Both novels will be used as sources of 'data' for ethical reflection. In this there will be much particularity, though I believe that general lessons can be extracted from the fate of these two characters.

My general position is that the human ethical sensibility works best when dealing with particular persons in specific contexts; abstract generalities are not the natural *modus operandi* of the moral sense. Partly because philosophy is so wedded to generalities, such moral *concreta* tend to be ignored—they are felt to be too saturated in detail: but this shows a naïve and oversimplified view of the relation between the particular and the general. One of the reasons we are drawn to fictional works is precisely that they combine the particular and the general in ways we find natural and intelligible. The general is woven into the particular, which gives the particular significance and the general substance. This point should become more evident when I come to discussing the works of fiction in question. It will then be clear that their themes are by no means lacking in philosophical content.

I shall also investigate a question of great interest to society at large but which is hardly ever considered by contemporary philosophers—the nature of evil.[4] In particular, I am interested in

---

[4] There is much journalistic interest in the topic, generally prompted by gruesome crimes of one sort or another. A discussion in this vein is Lyall Watson, *Dark Nature*.

the analysis and explanation of the evil character: what it consists in, what might underlie it, what might be done to remedy it. For all sorts of reasons, this is a question on which we badly need some illumination, or at least some conceptual apparatus that will help focus our thinking on the matter. My aim is to develop the outlines of a moral psychology of evil in which its structure is laid bare—an articulation of its mental architecture. This question fits neatly into neither metaethics nor normative ethics, as these are typically conceived. Yet it is surely a central question of anything deserving the name of ethics. And it is clearly a subject of intense interest to the novelist. The virtual absence of this subject from current moral philosophy should alert us to its parochiality.

Another theme to be discussed, also not easily slotted into the usual bipartite picture, is the relation between ethics and aesthetics. I do not mean the question of whether both sorts of concept should be treated in this or that way—as objective or subjective, say—but rather the question of how the two sorts of concept interpenetrate. How are beauty and goodness related, especially as they are exemplified in persons? This question arises in an arresting way in *The Picture of Dorian Gray*, in which an apparent conflict is set up between the two sorts of value; but I am also interested in the more general question of whether the ethical might in some sense be explicable in terms of the aesthetic. I approach this question by investigating the idea, by no means unfamiliar in the general culture and backed by a long and rich tradition, that goodness of character is identifiable with beauty of soul. Despite its distinguished history and wide popular acceptance, this is an idea that has been neglected by academic moral philosophy.[5] There ought, at least, to be some intellectual space in which we can discuss it. As will emerge, I believe it to be an idea with considerable plausibility and intrinsic interest.

In addition to these *outré* topics, I shall also discuss some questions more familiar in the analytical tradition. These questions might be seen as necessary preliminaries to the other topics, in the sense that we need to have some idea about the general status

---

[5] A notable exception is Robert E. Norton, *The Beautiful Soul*. Norton is, however, a German scholar, not a moral philosopher. I was greatly surprised (and pleased) when his book appeared, as I had supposed that no one else but me was interested in the topic. It is, moreover, an excellent historical study.

of moral discourse before we can use it to handle those other questions. We need, in particular, to assure ourselves that the concept of moral *knowledge* can be placed on a secure foundation—and this will require us to get clear about *what* it is that is known when a moral judgement is formed. In short, we need to establish that moral discourse is a fit subject for serious theoretical application. I shall therefore be criticizing certain positions that purport to undermine the robustness and objectivity of moral judgement. I want, among other things, to clear the way for a confident unapologetic use of moral notions in application to my later topics by defending a strongly objectivist or 'cognitivist' view of moral truth. In pursuance of this I shall oppose the idea that ethical knowledge is somehow inferior to scientific knowledge, perhaps to the point of not even deserving the epithet 'knowledge'. I shall also oppose the notion that moral properties are reducible to mental properties of some sort, putting in its place a wholly non-psychologistic conception of moral properties. Here is where the book will be most metaphysical in its concerns, and closest to contemporary academic discussions. Readers with little taste for this (or those already accustomed to using moral language without the distancing device of implicit quotation marks) may wish to skim these opening chapters and resume closer reading for the later, less abstract chapters.[6]

So some of the book will be business as usual, while some will be unusual business. My larger hope is to persuade the reader that ethics needs to range widely and variously if it is to have the kind of depth and interest we seek in it. This is accordingly a self-consciously synoptic or eclectic work, mixing metaphysics, epistemology, psychology, literature, film, and personal experience. As so often, we should not let our field of operations be limited by the methods and style recommended by some prevailing paradigm; we need to adopt new methods and develop new styles in response to the topics that ought to engage our attention. Ontology first; then figure out the appropriate methodology. The notion of rigour is topic-sensitive, so that the standards appropri-

---

[6] I do believe, however, that it is important to have some articulate grasp of the general nature of moral discourse when undertaking serious ethical discussions, if only to ward off the ill effects of implicit bad philosophy. Hence the practical value of metaethics. In moral philosophy, the theoretical and the applied are not really separable.

ate to one area may not carry over to another. Certainly, we should not neglect important ethical questions simply because their pursuit will not look much like some chosen paradigm of the rigorous—say, physics or logic or linguistics or historical scholarship. In this book I have been guided mainly by what strikes me as *interesting*, without worrying too much about how to relate what I have to say to orthodox analytical ethics (not that I regard that discipline as without interest, by any means). I suppose I do think that philosophical ethics should be more exciting than it tends to be—because questions of good and evil are among the most engaging of questions. This then is my attempt to make what strikes me as ethically vital into something feasible as an object of philosophical study; I have sought to convert some of my own ethical preoccupations into something recognizable as philosophy.

The danger in philosophical ethics is that what we gain in philosophical precision we lose in intrinsic interest, and conversely. The task is to develop a moral philosophy that is both philosophically substantial and which also engages our real ethical concerns. No doubt there will always be some distance between these two regions of human concern, but it should be possible to bring them into closer alignment than has been customary. In this way, philosophy might become a little less detached from life.[7]

---

[7] In the case of moral philosophy, there is a special obligation to connect philosophy with life, since life is where the moral life is lived (if I may be excused the tautology). Moral conceptions completely permeate the experience of living—what it is like to be a rational human being. Literature deals supremely with human life as it is lived, and morality is woven into life at every point. An adequate moral philosophy must find a way to articulate the concept of a moral life; it is not enough simply to set out a list of moral issues.

2

Goodness

1. MORAL PSYCHOLOGISM

What sort of property is the property of moral goodness? What does it consist in for something to be good? It has been very commonly assumed, or contended, that goodness is in some way analysable as a *psychological* property of some sort. The most prominent and plausible version of this thesis holds that for something to be good is for certain attitudes to be held towards it—attitudes of endorsement or approval or esteem.[1] Moral values are thus deemed subjective, in the sense that they are the upshot of mental states of subjects. Goodness is constituted, ultimately, by our consciousness of it. Morality is accordingly internal to the mind, metaphysically speaking. It is, if you like, a projection of our psychological nature.

In this chapter I shall argue against this thesis of moral psychologism. The property of moral goodness, I shall argue, is an objective property in the sense that it is constituted independently of any mental fact. I shall also be concerned to articulate precisely *why* it is that moral psychologism is false, and show what follows from its falsity. Readers already convinced that goodness is not a psychological property may then find some interest in tracing out the underlying reasons for its not being so.

I have asked what sort of property goodness is, but there is a whole tradition in moral philosophy dedicated to the proposition that it is no sort of property at all—that it is a pseudo-property.[2]

---

[1] This idea goes back to David Hume, at least: *Treatise of Human Nature*. Adherents of the position are too numerous to cite. Perhaps the most general formulation of the idea is that goodness is what we *find* to be good—what *impresses* us as good. I mean to be discussing the most general possible interpretation of the position, not some specific version of it.

[2] I get this commendably forthright phrase from A. J. Ayer's discussion of

This is the so-called non-cognitivist tradition, which holds that moral utterances are not fact-stating, do not admit of truth and falsity, denote no genuine moral properties that things can have or fail to have. Instead they are merely 'expressive' of the feelings and attitudes of speakers. I shall not discuss such views fully here. They are motivated largely by the perceived failure of the objectivist position I will defend, so that if that position can be rendered plausible there will be no need to contemplate the kind of revisionism entailed by the non-cognitivist thesis. I also think that much of what is appealing about the thesis is already contained in the subjectivist view of moral properties, since both locate the source of morality in the psychological states of subjects. Besides, non-cognitivism does not avoid the problem of saying what sort of property goodness is, since the attitudes it invokes must always contain the concept *good* as part of their content or else fail to constitute a genuinely moral evaluation. The emotion I express by saying 'That is good' will be an emotion of approval, but that is an emotion in whose content the concept of goodness occurs—it is the feeling *that* something is good. If we now try to explain this concept by appeal to other emotions and attitudes expressed by moral words, we generate an infinite regress, since these further psychological states will have to have the concept of goodness built into them too, on pain of not constituting *moral* attitudes. The problem is that if goodness is a pseudo-concept then it cannot serve to give the content of a psychological state, but if it cannot do that then the non-cognitivist runs out of resources with which to characterize morality. Moving from the assertoric form of speech to the optative or imperative or some such does not avoid the property of goodness; it simply crops up in the psychological states that underlie these utterances when they are intended morally. So no flight from the property of goodness is entailed by shifting from beliefs to non-cognitive mental states. The entire non-cognitivist tradition is a red herring from the point of view of explicating what the property of goodness is, since that property has not been eliminated from the materials it allows itself. Non-cognitivism is orthogonal to the dispute about

ethical propositions in *Language, Truth and Logic*, ch. 6. Ayer's exposition of the emotivist theory strikes me as still the clearest and most ingenuous available.

what kind of property goodness is, and so cannot be deployed as a way to side-step that question. I shall proceed, then, on the assumption that goodness is *some* sort of property—which I take to be the common-sense position. So let us agree that there is my mental act of judging that something is good, on the one hand, and there are the intentional objects of this act, on the other— whatever I am referring to together with the property of goodness I am attributing to it. My judgement is then true if and only if the former has the latter. The question is what sort of thing this property of goodness *is* that I attribute. Is it a property that is somehow constituted by our psychological responses to things?

The most promising version of the subjectivist thesis is that goodness is a *dispositional* property of a certain sort.[3] In order to make moral properties both applicable to external things and yet psychologically constituted, they are construed as dispositions on the part of *objects* to elicit psychological responses in *subjects*. The natural model here is colours: objects have dispositions to appear in certain ways to perceivers, and this is what their having colours consists in. Thus, for something to be good is for it to be disposed to elicit in people the judgement that it is good or some attitude of approval or positive emotion. There are many versions of this basic idea, but what unites them is the thesis that moral properties hold in virtue of relations to psychological subjects. Thus the property I judge something to have when I judge it to be good is the property of being disposed to make me and others judge that something has that property: it is a self-referential property. On this view, then, there is an internal relation between moral properties and moral reactions—when you analyse the properties you find elements of mind embedded in them. This is a view that purports to locate moral properties in the natural world of human psychology, and hence to offer a non-mysterious metaphysics and epistemology of morals. Let us now enquire into the plausibility of this analysis.

---

[3] I discuss such a theory, unfavourably, in *The Subjective View*, ch. 8. Recent notable discussions are David Lewis, Mark Johnston, and Michael Smith, 'Dispositional Theories of Value'; and John McDowell, 'Values and Secondary Qualities'.

2. THE NATURALISTIC FALLACY?

The first and most obvious problem is that the view commits the naturalistic fallacy: it tries to deduce a moral 'ought' from the natural facts of human psychology.[4] Let me put the point this way. If a state of affairs *S* is good, then it follows that we ought to promote *S*, simply in virtue of the meanings of these words: 'good' and 'ought' are logically related. This, though obvious, is a highly significant semantic fact: 'good' makes no apparent reference to agents or prescriptions to action, but it *entails* a form of words that *does* make precisely these references. You can *deduce* a statement about agents and their prescribed actions just from the proposition that a state of affairs has the monadic property of goodness. And this is definitive of the concept of goodness—part of what it contains. No analysis of that concept can be adequate, therefore, if it fails to yield this entailment. Call this, parodying Tarski's famous Convention T, Convention G. Convention T says that any adequate definition of truth must support—and not be incompatible with—the truth of biconditionals of the form 's is true if and only if p', where 's' names a sentence and 'p' repeats the content of that sentence: that is, these disquotational propositions are part of the meaning of 'true'.[5] Convention G, by analogy, says that any adequate definition of 'good' must respect biconditionals of the form 'S is good if and only if it ought (morally) to be the case that agents do *A*, if they can', where *S* is a state of affairs and *A* a type of action that promotes *S*. Instances of this G schema are logical truths, and hence failure to generate them shows that a purported definition of 'good' has failed to capture its meaning. Just as truth should be disquotational, so goodness should be ought-entailing.

Now the naturalistic fallacy, so called, arises when a purported definition of 'good' employs resources that are inherently

---

[4] The *locus classicus* is G. E. Moore, *Principia Ethica*. See especially the newly printed Preface to the second edition, in which Moore does much to clean up his earlier discussion of the naturalistic fallacy. I shall not here undertake a full-scale defence of Moore's basic point, taking it to be sufficiently well established and widely accepted. I think the general Moorean thesis is quite incontrovertible and absolutely essential to a sound philosophy of moral value.

[5] For a detailed exposition, see Alfred Tarski, 'The Concept of Truth in Formalised Languages'.

incapable of yielding instances of Convention G. And the objection to the dispositional thesis we are considering is that it fails to satisfy this demand. This is simply because from the mere fact that people are disposed to judge that *S* is good it does *not* follow that agents ought to promote *S*. What we need is the further proposition that this judgement is true, that is, that *S is* good. But that is to reintroduce in unanalysed form the very concept we are trying to explain. What follows from the original definition, at best, is that people *think* we ought to promote *S*, since they judge it to be good. But that is not Convention G, which requires that it *be* right to promote *S*, not that it be *thought* to be right. The problem, obviously, is that you cannot deduce from the fact that people are disposed to think we should promote *S* that we really ought to promote *S*. That would be like inferring from the fact that people are disposed to think that something is true that it really is true. The analogue would be a definition of truth that yielded instances of '*s* is true if and only if people are disposed to think that *p*', where '*p*' gives the content of '*s*'. It is likewise simply not part of the meaning of 'good' that we have instances of '*S* is good if and only if people think that we should promote *S*'. It is not merely that people can be wrong in what they think ought to be pursued; it is that the premiss is simply of the wrong logical type to yield the conclusion. To suppose otherwise is to elevate a straightforward *non sequitur* into a definition. The best that could come of this would be a stipulation of a new meaning for the word 'good', not an analysis of what it now means.

Notice that this problem does not apply to the case of colour because colour terms are not evaluative terms, and so no attempt to reduce the evaluative to the non-evaluative is afoot. There is no Convention C telling us that any adequate definition of colour must guarantee that if something has a given colour then we ought to promote its existence! The disanalogy in this respect is enough to undermine any effort to treat goodness as logically on a par with colour.[6]

This objection seems to me decisive against psychologically

---

[6] Although I rejected the analogy between colour and value in *The Subjective View*, I did not explicitly link this to the naturalistic fallacy. It now seems to me that this is the decisive point.

reductive dispositional theories, but it is possible to be a non-reductive dispositionalist.[7] One might hold that to be good is to be morally valued in accordance with the dictates of moral reason: goodness is what sound practical reason favours. Here the disposition is constrained by certain normative standards, so that it looks as if we have the kind of analysis from which it will be *possible* to derive the requisite ought-statements, since surely if sound moral reason favours something then it ought to be pursued. No naturalistic fallacy will be committed because we shall have injected normative content into the analysis. So it might seem as if we can have a form of psychologism about goodness that preserves its ought-implications: we make essential reference to moral psychology in giving conditions for something to be good, while requiring that the resulting judgements meet certain normative standards. It is not the mere fact of people judging something to be good that constitutes goodness but rather their doing so in ways that respect moral rationality.

We should first note how analytically unambitious this view is. It does not attempt to explain or analyse moral notions, since it frankly uses them in the specification of the disposition. Moral norms are kept in unreduced form. But now there is the question what the point of the analysis is: why not just leave goodness in unreduced form in the simple way and forego the dispositional treatment? Something is good if and only if it is *good*, not if and only if moral reason favours it. Moral reason favours it because it is good, surely, so we have not found anything more fundamental on which to base goodness. If norms are to be left unreduced why not leave them unreduced at the start?

To this it may be replied that at least we are avoiding postulating values in the world—goodness as a property of states of affairs—by using normative notions only in characterizing pieces of reasoning. So we don't have queer non-causal unexplanatory properties out there posing an ontological embarrassment; we just have moral reason and the standards proper to it. But, first, we don't really avoid the alleged ontological queernesss this way because we still have normative notions being applied to reason-

---

[7] This is in effect the position adopted by Mark Johnston in Lewis, Johnston, and Smith, 'Dispositional Theories of Value'. I am grateful to him for discussions of his theory.

ing, and these notions are no more causally explanatory here than they are when applied to states of affairs. If I form a thought or desire that is required by morality, then this property—being required by morality—is still not a naturalistic property of the thought or desire. The case is really no different, fundamentally, from what follows if moral properties always ultimately apply to mental states—as it might be, pleasure and pain. The property that pleasure has of being good is not a naturalistic explanatory property of pleasure; but then neither is the property of an emotion's being morally appropriate or a desire's being morally required or a belief's being morally justified. Moral norms are simply not part of the empirical world of cause and effect, wherever they crop up. The dispositional theory simply shifts them inwards, hoping they will appear less queer once safely in the mind. It is the same with logical norms: they too apply to thoughts without being naturalistic properties of them. Of course, we might try to make these norms go away by offering some reductive naturalistic account of them. But that will just take us back to the original objection that we can't derive an 'ought' from such an analysis of goodness. So we need to keep the norms in somewhere, and the point is that they are no more ontologically innocuous when predicated of the mind than when predicated of the world. Just as being logically valid is a feature of reasoning that lacks causal-explanatory force, so is being recommended by moral reason; it is nothing other than the property of being such that you *ought* morally to think it or desire it. The 'ought' here is no more naturalistic than the simple unreduced 'good' when applied to states of affairs.

Secondly, why is it a worry that moral properties play no role in fixing how the world works? Why is this a count against them, a reason to doubt their existence? It is true enough that they lack such a causal-empirical role, but doesn't that just tell us what *kind* of property they are, not that they cannot exist? Whence the dogma that the real is coterminous with the causal? Mathematics is an obvious problem for this criterion, notoriously so. Consider the property of being explanatory itself: is *this* property explanatory of anything? The property of being square explains why the peg won't fit into a round hole, but what does this property of being explanatory explain? If we make explanatory power the sole test of a property's legitimacy, then even explanatoriness is not a legitimate property—which has the look of a self-refuting position. And then there is the whole range of evaluative epistemic properties—being justified, validly deduced, reasonable, and so on. Goodness is just one among many properties that don't figure in causal explanations. (I shall say more about this in the next chapter.)

There is in any case something perverse about requiring moral properties to have causal-explanatory power. It amounts to a sort of category mistake. Moral properties imply evaluations and hence tell us what we ought to strive for—so says Convention G. There would be no point in that if they also told us what *will* or *might* actually happen—if they had some predictive explanatory force. Suppose '*S* is good' implied '*S* is likely to happen by dint of nomological necessity'. Then goodness would naturally lead to what we ought to bring about, independently of our will. But then it would not be the evaluative and prescriptive notion it is. It is in the very nature of goodness as evaluative and action-guiding that it *not* have implications for how things will go on independently of what we might do. The word 'good' is used to evaluate possible states of affairs with a view to deciding which we ought to bring about; it is not used to ascribe a property to things that will make things happen irrespective of what we decide. It is not that it somehow pretends to have this kind of causal role but philosophical reflection shows that it cannot fulfil it; rather, it is written into the notion that it *not* have such a job. If it turned out, *per impossibile*, to have such a role, then we would have to invent a new word that does the job of action-guiding evaluation. The non-causal character of the property of goodness is precisely what is needed in an evaluative concept, since the concept is directed to what ought to happen, not to what will happen. It would be utterly bizarre if goodness could, just by its instantiation in states of affairs, bring about effects in the world that do not go via our attitudes and actions; not because it is somehow culpably idle but simply because it is what it is—an evaluative notion. We read off from the property what *we* ought to do; we don't use it to make predictions of what will happen anyway. This is the great contrast between moral properties and naturalistic properties. It is part of the *essence* of goodness that it doesn't have the kind of explanatory role that empirical properties have. (This is one respect in which the analogy with mathematical properties is imperfect, since they do not have this normative essence. The *reason* for their causal inertia is not the same as that for moral properties: mathematical properties are, as it were, brutely non-causal, while ethical properties are non-causal on principle.)

This intuitive point can be bolstered with an argument by *reductio*. Suppose goodness were a naturalistic disposition with certain characteristic effects on the course of nature. These effects will themselves have to be good, or bad, or neutral. Then consider these in turn. If good, then goodness *pre-empts* us from doing what we ought—for it does good things by itself. So the 'ought' component of goodness would be otiose; good effects would be overdetermined by the world and our actions. If goodness had the power to produce good states of affairs, then what point would there be in deciding, on the strength of its application, that *we* ought to produce good states of affairs? 'Ought' implies 'may not': it cannot be the case that I ought to produce a certain state of affairs if that state of affairs will be produced by nature anyway. Goodness could not usurp the role of agents in increasing its distribution. If it could do that, then it would not entail obligations—which is to say, it would not be goodness.

It is no use to say here that goodness might have *some* natural powers to produce good states of affairs and some (other) ought-requirements that are up to moral agents, so that the concept could be introduced on the basis of its causal powers consistently with having the ought-implications. This is no use because that would only get us a thinned-down moral notion that coincides with the specified causal powers; there would still be an aspect to the concept that had no causal basis. This aspect would be open to the same demand to establish its causal credentials or get eliminated as an objective feature of the world. All we could save on a causal basis would be a putative aspect of the notion of goodness that had no ought-implications, but that would be enough to disqualify the concept from being a moral concept, since the ought-implications are definitive of the moral. 'Ought' implies 'will not happen independently of the will', so any causal powers to produce good effects will not belong to the 'ought' component. Thus if goodness could cause goodness by itself, then it would not be goodness, since it would not tell us what *we* ought to produce.

If the effects of goodness were bad, on the other hand, then good things could have bad effects—in which case we ought *not* to promote them. If goodness were a natural disposition to produce bad effects, then it would not be a property whose distribution we ought to increase—in which case it could not be goodness either.

If neutral, finally, then we should be morally indifferent to the effects of goodness. But how can we be indifferent to the effects of something to which we are not indifferent? Surely if it is rational to be indifferent to the effects of a property, then it should be rational to be indifferent to that property. But that would mean being indifferent to goodness, which is absurd.

Since these are the only options, then, it is absurd to suppose that goodness might be a natural disposition. There is nothing it could be a disposition *to* that makes it come out as the property it is. Consider, to drive the point home, an (im)possible world in which goodness has the natural propensity to produce just those effects that in the actual world we think it ought to encourage *us* to produce—it does by itself just what we ought to do. And why shouldn't this be a logically available world, given the hypothesis that goodness might be *some* kind of natural disposition? Then in that world moral agency becomes entirely pointless and the normative component of the concept is completely idle: there is simply nothing we ought to do in that world, morally speaking, since it is all done for us by goodness itself. But surely that is precisely a description of a world in which the property in question is not a moral property at all but some other natural property with remarkably benificent consequences. It is a world in which the laws of nature are geared to maximizing moral value independently of what anyone might will. Since it is an ought-free world, it is a world without moral properties. The putatively causal moral properties are not *moral* properties at all. Therefore there is no conceptually possible world of the kind in question. So the supposition that goodness might be a natural disposition refutes itself.

What we see here is that the non-causal character of moral properties is directly linked to their evaluative nature: you can *derive* the former from the latter. We might then say that moral properties are non-causal *de jure* while certain other non-causal properties are so only *de facto*—colour properties and mathematical properties, for instance. For we have a kind of proof from the evaluative nature of moral properties that they could not have causal powers. We should therefore not be alarmed that they lack causal powers; we should regard it as a natural consequence of their evaluative essence. According to many naturalistic reductions, goodness turns out to have causal powers, since the property with which it is identified has causal powers (happiness, for example); but it is precisely because of this that these reductions commit the naturalistic fallacy, and ignore the evaluative content of the concept. It is really a condition of adequacy on any account of goodness that causal powers *not* be conferred on it. The methodological lesson here is this: it is misguided to insist on a criterion of objective reality for properties that has the result that if the condition were met then the properties in question would not even *be* the properties they are. You cannot criticize moral properties for failing to pass a test which, had they passed it, would disqualify them from being moral properties. Since they are non-causal *de jure* it is misguided to bemoan the fact of their causal indolence. This is a sure symptom of judging all types of properties by the standards that are properly applicable only to some. That is why it is really quite inappropriate even to *venture* the idea that moral properties might be introduced by way of inference to the best causal explanation.[8] A category mistake has already been committed thereby. It is like asking colour properties to pass the test of not *looking* any way, or demanding that shape properties play *no* role in determining how the world works. The proposed test is not merely tendentious; it is incoherent once spelled out. Naturalistic moral properties would be 'queer' indeed.

It is often said that non-causal properties are epistemically problematic: we can give no decent account of how we come to think and know about them. I shall discuss this fully in the next chapter; for now, I want simply to point out that the dispositional account of goodness does not alleviate the alleged problem. It might seem that it does, since when I think and know about goodness I am intentionally directed towards a disposition to produce mental states of a certain sort, and mental states are the kinds of things that have causal powers. But this misses an

---

[8] See the well-known discussion by Gilbert Harman, *The Nature of Morality*, ch. 1. I criticize Harman's argument more fully in the next chapter.

important point: when I think about these mental states I need to have the concept of goodness in the content of my thought, since that concept occurs in the specification of the disposition. If good is being disposed to be judged good, then when I think 'This is good', I think 'This is disposed to be judged good'; but then I must be able to make a judgement that has the property of being good as its object, albeit as the object of someone else's judgement. The point is that the puzzles of moral intentionality are not avoided by this kind of analysis; they are just shifted. It is no use in avoiding the puzzle of how I make a judgement about goodness to say that goodness consists in people in general judging that something is good; we still have the question of how *this* works, and also of how I judge that it is *goodness* that they are judging about. And once moral intentionality is presupposed it is hard to see how we could take seriously any other epistemic worry about moral properties. Surely, if we are allowed to have unexplained thoughts about goodness, we must also be allowed to have unexplained justified beliefs and knowledge about goodness. Indeed, a weak and innocuous principle links intentionality with knowledge: namely, that if you can have a given property as the content of your thought then you can know at least in principle that the property is instantiated (barring radical scepticism). But this means that any theory that presupposes moral intentionality is presupposing moral knowledge, so it is not possible to motivate dispositional psychologism by way of the idea that moral properties are epistemically problematic. It is not possible, since buried in the theory is an occurrence of 'good' in an intentional context. If the non-causal character of the property of goodness is what is held to generate the epistemological problems that motivate dispositionalism, then we are not in a significantly better position if that property still occurs as the object of judgement.

There is, in sum, a difficult dilemma for the dispositional theorist of goodness: go reductive and lose the connections to 'ought' that define the concept of goodness, or retain a normative component in the analysis and then face the question of what is gained by the dispositional theory. In either case, the theory seems to have inverted the correct logical priorities. The relation between goodness and moral judgement is just that goodness is the property that moral judgement tracks; it is not that that property *consists* in being judged to obtain. The concept of goodness is prior to judgements of goodness; so there is no prospect of reversing the order of dependence and saying that goodness is to be explicated in terms of moral judgement. Moral reason should be defined as the faculty that generates judgements about goodness, rather than goodness being defined as what the moral faculty concerns. When I judge something to be good by exercising my moral reason I do not make a judgement about my moral reason, to the effect that it is operating optimally or some such. Rather, I ascribe a property whose identity is independent of the faculty I employ to track it. It is the *object* of my judgement, not a disguised version of my judgement. I refer to nothing psychological when I use the word 'good'. This is why I can simultaneously utter the counterfactual: 'Even if people's moral psychology were quite different, issuing in contrary judgements, this would *still* be good.' Ordinary language does not mislead us about the kind of property goodness is.

But is there a hint of superstition involved in believing that the world contains values as well as natural facts? Is it perhaps that we are compelled to accept them but in so doing we expand our ontology with properties that are intrinsically peculiar? Are we stocking the universe with ontological oddities, weaving ethereal threads into its otherwise plain and sturdy fabric? The question here is whether there is any *pretheoretical* sense in which moral properties are intrinsically queer. Of course they may seem anomalous with respect to some tendentious (and optional) set of metaphysical beliefs. Relative to empiricist epistemology they are indeed anomalous, but then so are many other things—mathematics, modality, logic, and so on. Relative to a causal criterion of reality they are likewise beyond the pale, but again so are many items in apparent good standing. We need a reason to suppose that moral properties are not simply counterexamples to such monolithic viewpoints. Is there any way in which moral properties are queer in some more neutral sense? I cannot see that there is. I would say that, pretheoretically, *meaning* is queerer than goodness; it strikes one as odd even ahead of adopting any general metaphysical outlook. There is that odd kind of reaching out and inclusiveness, the difficulty of seeing how it is possible for mere sounds to carry significance, the proximity of powerful sceptical arguments.[9] Not for nothing did Wittgenstein focus on meaning as a source of philosophical superstition; goodness seems sober by comparison. The self is pretty elusive as we pretheoretically conceive it. Free will is hardly dull. In fact, a lot of things are rather queer when you think about it, and more intrinsically queer than goodness. That should not be a reason to reject them (I say more on this in the next chapter). My suspicion is that goodness only seems queer because it is what it is and not any other thing. If your model of a decent property is one that has no evaluative aspect, then goodness will seem exceptional; the cure for this is a more pluralistic view in which properties can have quite different sorts of essence. People have supposed that *existence* is a queer sort of property, partly because it is not like ordinary perceptible causal properties. But the right response to this is that existence is just *different* from other properties. When we list the properties of an object and add existence, we add something of a new type, and not something an empiricist can happily embrace. Goodness is like existence in belonging to a different category from such properties as colour, shape, mass, and so on. In both cases there is a tendency, in view of the uniqueness of the property, to try to reduce it to something more familiar: existence is being perceptible or located in space; goodness is a feeling of approval. But these analyses distort the concept beyond recognition, and are prompted by misplaced assimilation. The merely different gets branded as queer, unless it can assimilate itself to the majority. There is really nothing alarming about the property of goodness once prejudice has been set aside. It is no more an affront to common sense to say that kindness is good than that it is rare, and no protective gloss is felt to be needed for this statement.

3. RELATIVISM

The dispositional analysis also runs into trouble by tying goodness too closely to what people happen to judge: we get an unac-

---

[9] See Thomas Nagel's discussion of the puzzle of meaning in *What Does it All Mean?*; also McGinn: *Problems in Philosophy*, ch. 4. Queerness is really a mark of

ceptable relativism about goodness. Suppose there is a disease that causes intense pain in us and at the same time interferes with our rational faculties in such a way as to make us judge that pain is good (this might be seen as a very clever virus that discourages its victims from curing themselves). Or if you find it hard to believe that you could be in pain and judge this to be good, imagine that the disease causes pain only in animals but also causes *us* to judge that this animal pain is good. Consider the moment when the disease takes hold and after a period of pain, which hitherto we judged to be bad, we begin to judge it to be good. Suppose that all of us make this new judgement and that we now have a standing disposition so to judge. Should we say that the pain *becomes* good at that point? It does not change intrinsically, only our beliefs about it change. Aren't our beliefs now simply false, since pain is *not* good? It is just that this is a strange disease that derails our ability to make sound value judgements. Given that such a disease is surely logically possible, it cannot be that goodness is constituted by judged goodness. It can hardly be that the analysis of goodness shows that no such disease is possible. Suppose the disease next makes people start stealing and lying and cheating with all the usual ill effects, while also making us judge that this is all good. Isn't this a case of a disease causing a new kind of insanity rather than all these things *becoming* good? How, to put it simply, can bad things become good just by people taking them to be good? There is obviously a logical gap between *being* good and being *taken* to be good.

Here we see the relativism that comes with the dispositional analysis. In effect, it makes moral value a direct function of what people believe to be valuable. If one group judges something to be good and another judges it to be bad, the theory must say that both are right, since the thing has both dispositions. The only way to avoid this, clearly, is to invoke a notion of being good that is *independent* of moral reactions, so that we can say that one group is right and the other wrong because of what *is* good (or bad). But that is to give up the analysis: it is to evaluate the attitudes themselves by a standard that transcends them. This is, I know, a simple and familiar point, but no less cogent for that.

the philosophical, not a peculiarity of moral value. This is what J. L. Mackie so signally fails to appreciate in his discussion of queerness in *Ethics: Inventing Right and Wrong*, ch. 1.

There is a structural reason why the dispositional theory gives the wrong results in the disease case and generates an unacceptable relativism. This is that moral properties are supervenient on the natural intrinsic properties of states of affairs, but the corresponding dispositions to judge are not. Pain is bad in virtue of the intrinsic quality of pain, so that (other things being equal) the same degree of pain gives the same degree of disvalue. If two situations are exactly alike in degree of pain and other non-moral respects, then they are necessarily exactly alike with respect to value. But the disposition to *judge* that pain is bad cannot be necessitated simply by the intrinsic quality of pain: agents are not all necessarily going to judge that someone's pain is bad and vary their judgements of value according to the quality of the pain. For these judgements are *extrinsic* to the natural properties of the pain itself; hence the contingency of the link between them and the intrinsic nature of the pain. When I judge that your pain is bad, my judgement occurs outside the nexus of your pain, so there is room for the judgement to vary while the pain remains the same. But the value itself is not extrinsic in this way since it is strongly supervenient on the quality of the pain; there is no room for the value to vary while the pain stays the same. The value is far more *intrinsic* to the pain than the judgement is, which is why the former supervenes and the latter does not. Thus the dispositional theory has the problem that it has to deny the intrinsic supervenience of the moral on the natural—the idea that the only things we need to know about something in order to judge the value attaching to it are its inherent features. We do not need to look outside the object to see what responses it evokes elsewhere, since these are not part of the supervenience base for moral properties. Two situations can be exactly alike intrinsically in such a way as to confer the same value on them, even though they differ in the extrinsic responses they evoke in people. The dispositional theory is too externalist in its preferred supervenience base; it cannot allow that things have *intrinsic* value and hence exhibit *local* supervenience.[10] It is this error that lies behind the kind of relativism revealed by the disease case.

[10] This is one of the main points of Moore's seminal paper, 'The Conception of Intrinsic Value'.

4. LOGICAL PRIORITY AND THE
BICONDITIONALS

I have just argued that the biconditionals linking goodness with judgements of goodness are not necessary truths. The point I want to make now is that even if they were, this would not establish the dispositional theory of what goodness *is*. Suppose that it could not be the case that something is judged to be good without being good and vice versa. That is clearly not sufficient for it to be the case that goodness *is* the disposition to judge its presence: for the judgement might just be a necessary *consequence* of the moral property. It may be that moral properties covary with dispositions to judge of their presence, without it being true that they are constituted by such dispositions. It is true of pain that it is present if and only if the person suffering it judges that it is (more or less), but that does not lead to any collapse of pain into judgements about pain. It might indeed be that the pain is the *ground* of such a disposition, and is logically prior to it. Such biconditionals merely record a fact about the necessary relation between a property and people's propensity to detect its presence; they do not by themselves warrant the much stronger claim that the property just is the propensity. Every property can be seen to give rise in this way to a disposition to detect its presence, in certain specifiable conditions, but this hardly warrants any reductive gloss on the corresponding biconditionals. The moral dispositionalist needs to show that his biconditionals are more than just a special case of this perfectly universal truth. Not *all* properties are subjective or response-involving in his intended sense. Short of an outright assertion of reduction, the biconditionals are too weak to give the dispositionalist what he wants.

The most promising strategy for strengthening the biconditionals in a reductive direction is to show that the property in question is *relative* to the proffered psychological conditions. Thus in the case of colour we argue that, unlike shape, the colour of an object varies with the perceptual responses it evokes: in a possible world in which actually red objects systematically look green to perceivers, it is correct to call those objects green.[11] But

---

[11] For a defence of such relativism about colour, see McGinn, *The Subjective View*, esp. ch. 1.

this strategy is precisely what we don't want for the case of moral properties. So that way of saving the biconditionals from triviality is unavailable, and it is quite unclear what else might be brought in to shore them up. We should beware, then, of reading the biconditionals in a reductive style when they assert nothing of the kind.

5. A TEMPTING ERROR

Suppose we believe, not absurdly, that all value basically attaches to psychological states of some sort; and suppose we identify the crucial psychological state as that of taking pleasure in something. Then something will count as good if and only if we take pleasure in it. But taking pleasure in something involves favouring or preferring or approving it. So something is good just if we have these attitudes towards it, that is, if it disposes us to have such attitudes. And this sounds a lot like the dispositional thesis. So don't we have a route into that thesis from the assumption that all morally relevant facts are psychological? No, we do not. This argument confuses (among other things) the bearer of goodness with the analysis of goodness. Let it be true that pleasure is the only good; it does not follow that its *being* good reduces to pleasure. I judge *of* pleasure that it is good, but that is not to say that 'good' *means* 'pleasure'. The crucial step in the argument moves from taking pleasure in something to favouring it, or taking it to be valuable. But this is a real logical step, not a mere repetition of the ascription of pleasure. There are two attitudes involved here, which the argument wrongly conflates: the attitude of taking pleasure in something, and the attitude that judges pleasure to be good. It may be true that finding pleasure in something is the only thing that is good, but it does not follow that moral approval *is* the taking of pleasure. It may even be true that moral approval is always a form of pleasure, but that is not to say that there is nothing more to it than pleasure; all that follows is that we can say that moral approval itself is one of the goods, since it is an instance of pleasure. No defence of the dispositionalist thesis can be derived from the supposed truth that dispositions to give pleasure are the only good. Even if the only good were the pleasurable moral approval of things, it would not follow that the goodness of this consisted in moral approval.

A related error is to suppose that the supervenience of the moral on the psychological implies that moral properties are themselves psychological properties. Suppose we start with the idea that value supervenes solely on the psychological aspects of situations. Goodness is thus logically necessitated by psychological facts; any other facts are irrelevant. Then, certainly, we have an exceptionally tight link between moral and mental properties. It might now be carelessly supposed that moral properties must be in some way mental. But of course that does not follow; supervenience is mere necessary covariation of properties, not reduction of them. Supervenience of the mental on the physical does not imply that the mental *is* the physical. So it is perfectly consistent to assert a strong dependence of the moral on the mental and yet deny that goodness is in any way a mental property. Indeed, its evaluative nature, as enshrined in Convention G, precludes such a reduction. Still, I would not be at all surprised if the tight link with the mental entailed by supervenience subliminally inclined people towards ethical psychologism, confused as this would be. Thinking vaguely that moral distinctions are constituted by mental distinctions, as supervenience asserts, one moves to the thesis that there is no more to moral properties than their mental bases. The corresponding move in the case of the mental and the physical should help inoculate one against this *non sequitur*. The essential point to remember in the moral case is that moral concepts evaluate while mental concepts do not; supervenience of the former on the latter does not erase this categorial distinction.

6. MORAL INTENTIONALITY

Let us now enquire into the structure of moral intentionality—what it is like to think about the property of goodness. There are peculiarities here that help explain—though they do not serve to justify—the attraction of mentalistic conceptions of the moral. We shall see that these peculiarities can be explained in other terms.

It is natural to suppose that there is an especially intimate connection between goodness and thoughts about it. It can seem that the nature of goodness is exhausted by the mental act of grasping it: the property seems fully present to the mind. The dispositional theory construes this as reflecting the fact that the property can be analysed in terms of appropriate mental acts. But it is possible to accept the internality of the relation without collapsing the property into the attitude: one can be an *externalist* about the content of moral judgement.[12] That is, the property itself, though not in any way mental, nevertheless individuates attitudes towards it. The property of goodness occurs as a *constituent* of moral thoughts. Moral intentionality thus exhibits the kind of ontological dependence upon its object that externalism generally maintains. This inverts the order of dependence claimed by the dispositionalist: it is not that goodness is constituted by thoughts about goodness; rather, the thoughts themselves are (partly) constituted by the non-mental property of goodness. This begins to explain why it is sometimes felt that there is no real distinction between the moral property and the judgement, but it does so without compromising the objectivity of the property.

But now this raises an interesting question: why isn't there the same sort of psychologizing tendency in the case of other sorts of property, given that externalism is generally true of content? Why don't people tend to think that water is subjective on the grounds that water individuates thoughts about water? A similar question can be raised about mathematics: there is a psychologizing tendency there too, but how can this be diagnosed as arising from a mistaken reaction to the truth of externalism, if externalism provokes no such tendency in other cases? The answer is that there are certain relevant differences between the cases. The structure of the intentional act differs in the moral and mathematical case from its structure in the case of empirical properties. There are three types of difference to note.

First, moral properties, as we have said, lack causal powers. The only way in which they can influence the course of events is if they are represented by some subject—if they are judged to apply. Then they can sometimes play a very large causal role. But then there can be no distinction between the causal powers of the

---

[12] I discuss externalism at length in *Mental Content*. In the terminology employed there, moral content is *weakly* external: objective goodness individuates moral thoughts, but it is not possible to vary moral content simply by altering what holds in the thinker's environment.

property itself and the causal powers of judgements about it—
the two cannot be distinguished by their having different causal
powers. This makes the case different from beliefs about natural
kinds like water, since water clearly has a quite distinct set of
causal powers from that of beliefs about it (water can dissolve
salt, but beliefs about water can't). Moreover, this is evident in
the very act of thinking about water, since its causal powers will
tend to be known by the thinker, or at least he will know that he
is thinking about the *kind* of thing that has independent causal
powers. Not so in the case of thoughts about goodness. But given
this asymmetry, it is perhaps not surprising that we feel a robust
distinctness of property and thought in one case but not in the
other. Divergent causal profiles ground the distinction for water
but not for goodness. In the case of goodness the only causal
power attaches to the thought, so, assuming a causal conception
of properties, we are apt to think that only one property is in
play—the property of thinking about goodness. Thus we end up
saying that water is objective while goodness is not. (The same
kind of point applies to mathematical properties.) But it would
be a mistake to take this difference as a good *argument* for subjectivism; rather, it simply points to a basic distinction between
moral and physical properties. My point is that in the light of this
difference with respect to causal powers we can see how people
might erroneously conclude that moral properties have no existence apart from attitudes towards them. The right conclusion is
simply that moral properties have no causal powers, so we cannot ground their distinctness from thoughts by drawing attention
to the way their causal powers differ from those of thoughts.

Second, natural kinds exhibit an appearance–reality distinction that moral properties do not. A natural kind like water is presented to the senses in various ways, and we recognize that these
distinct presentations are all appearances of the same property.
There are many subjective appearances of a single objective type.
But in the moral case it does not work like this, since moral properties do not present different appearances to the senses. In their
case, we just grasp the property 'directly', without mediation by
an appearance: it shows up in our judgements naked, just as it is.
As Locke would say, it has only a nominal essence.[13] But then,

---

[13] John Locke, *Essay Concerning Human Understanding*, esp. ch. VI.

again, it is intelligible that this should be wrongly interpreted as a reason to doubt the objectivity of the property, since we cannot explain its objectivity by invoking the appearance–reality distinction. We cannot say that it is what lies behind its various appearances; it just *is* what appears. We cannot ground its mind-independence by pointing to the distance between its subjective appearances to the mind and what it is in itself. But this is not to say that goodness collapses into subjectivity; rather, the objective property of goodness individuates our grasp of it—the property is immediately given in moral intentionality. This peculiarity of moral intentionality should therefore not be construed as an indication of the subjectivity of goodness.

Third, precisely because of this unmediated presence we cannot form the idea of a vehicle–content distinction in the moral case. In the empirical cases, it at least looks (however confusedly) as if we can do this, because we can treat the appearance aspect as the vehicle for the objective content. The subjective appearance of water, say, acts as the vehicle for thoughts about the objective thing. This gives us the idea that the object of thought transcends the subjective—it is what is borne by the vehicle. But moral properties do not suggest this way of thinking, since there is nothing to hand that could function as a vehicle that stands apart from the content itself. It is as if the property must be its own vehicle. And this makes it look as if it must be a denizen of the mind. But the right thing to say here is that the vehicle–content distinction, so understood, has no purchase in the moral case, even if it does in other cases. The moral property simply constitutes the content and there is no further intrinsic feature that the judgement has.

These points show that moral intentionality is significantly different from other kinds, and thus explain why it is that the truth of externalism might tempt one in a psychologistic direction. The internality of the relation between thought and object is being taken the wrong way round, but for intelligible reasons. What we should say is that the non-mental property of goodness occurs as a constituent of moral judgements, not that the property is mental because dependent on those judgements.

7. PSYCHOLOGISM AND MORAL ENQUIRY

If moral properties were psychological properties, then they would show the characteristic features of the mental. Mental properties have both a first-person and a third-person aspect: they are introspectible by their subject and attributable to others on the basis of their behaviour. They also function in the explanation of behaviour, presumably causally. But when I attribute goodness to something—an act or a person or a state of affairs—I surely do not attribute a property with these features. The property attributed is neither introspectible nor explanatory of behaviour. I do not ascribe it either by introspecting its presence in myself (I may not be at all good!) or by seeing the need of it to explain what somebody else did. Moral properties are simply not part of psychology. Psychology is an empirical science, employing a domain of explanatory properties, and tested by its empirical success. But goodness is an evaluative property that plays no role in psychological theory. When I judge something to be good I do not thereby ascribe any mental property to anyone. That is why we do not ask for the introspective or explanatory justification for such an ascription. These would be quite inappropriate questions. We do not decide upon the truth-value of a moral statement by investigating psychological subjects to see what is going on in them. Moral methods of discovery are not psychological methods. But they would have to be if any version of moral psychologism were correct.

The point here is exactly analogous to a classic point made against psychologism in logic: namely, that if it were true, then the correct method of logical discovery would be empirical psychological investigation—yet surely logical knowledge is not acquired in this way.[14] If it were, then it would be vulnerable to revisions of psychological theory: logical laws would be hostage to the empirical fortunes of psychological hypotheses. In the same way, if moral enquiry depended upon psychological information, then we would have to revise our ethical beliefs if psychology turned out differently from what we had supposed. Indeed, we would have to wait for the psychological information

---

[14] This anti-psychologistic point, among others, is made by Edmund Husserl in *Logical Investigations*, i. 144 f.

to be gathered before we could venture a moral judgement, since every moral judgement would be an empirical psychological hypothesis. So, right now, we have to say that it could turn out that murder is right, since the psychological generalization that people disapprove of murder is empirically falsifiable. This is simply because what people *think* to be right is an empirical matter, to be determined by the usual kind of inference to the best explanation; but that is not how we regard the question of whether something *is* right. That question is to be decided, roughly speaking, by its consonance with basic moral principle. The case is exactly analogous to our assent to *modus ponens*: it is an empirical matter whether people reason in accordance with that principle, but that is not the reason why we accept it as logically valid. Therefore it is not reducible to a statement of empirical psychology. Neither the logician nor the moralist proceeds by conducting empirical inquiries into people's contingent psychology.

Furthermore, if goodness were a mental property, then scepticism about mental properties would imply scepticism about moral properties. Eliminativism in psychology would entail eliminativism in ethics, since if there are no desires or judgements there aren't the mental states that are held to define goodness. The dispositional theory must assume that eliminativism in psychology is false. No doubt it is, but morals should not depend on this. Less extremely, suppose that scepticism about mental content is true, so that no one succeeds in meaning or judging anything; then we get the result that there cannot be moral truths either.[15] If no belief or desire can have determinate content, then neither can those beliefs and desires that are held to constitute goodness—so goodness vanishes with them. The semantic sceptic has inadvertently shown that nothing is right or wrong, as well as that nobody believes or desires anything. The only way to avoid this result is to reject psychologism about value. We surely do not want to conclude that pain isn't bad just because no belief about pain could have content, as some sceptical views about content imply. Philosophy of mind doesn't have this kind of bearing on ethics; it is autonomous relative to such questions.

[15] For an exposition of semantic scepticism, see Saul Kripke, *Wittgenstein on Rules and Private Language*. The implications of such scepticism for ethics, under a subjectivist interpretation, seem never to have been remarked upon—though they are clearly devastating. Objectivist ethical views have no such vulnerability.

8. THE ESSENCE OF GOODNESS

We have seen that goodness is not a mental property. The question then is what sort of property it is: what are the truth conditions of moral judgements—how is 'good' to be analysed? This is a dangerous question, however, if intended in a certain way—as asking for an explication of goodness in *other terms*. Such a question is often asked against the background of some presumed metaphysics which recognizes only certain categories of properties, and the question is which of these categories the properties in question belong to. Thus we might recognize only mental and physical properties, and then the question is which of these moral properties are to be: if not one, then the other. But we should resist such procrusteanism: the right answer is that goodness is a *moral* property, neither more nor less. It is not some other kind of property in disguise—mental, physical, or other. It is what it is—a separate type of property.

That is not to say we can say nothing about it. We have already said that goodness is evaluative, non-causal, and supervenient on natural properties; and we have explained some of the links between these features. But these remarks are not intended as a *definition* of goodness, an attempt to give non-circular necessary and sufficient conditions; they merely record some of the essential characteristics of moral properties. I take it that the concept is indefinable in any interesting sense; it is a conceptual primitive. Perhaps some of the drive towards psychologism arises from a desire for definition at whatever price—in which case the cure is to acknowledge that all definition has its limits.

G. E. Moore famously described goodness as simple, unanalysable, and non-natural.[16] We can agree with the spirit of his description while having some misgivings about its letter. Goodness is non-natural if that means that it is neither mental nor material, and hence non-causal. But, as I indicated earlier, it is not non-natural in any juicier sense—as, say, poltergeists and angels are. The property of goodness is part of plain common sense, not a piece of speculative parascience or religious metaphysics. It is also unanalysable in any non-moral terms, though it may well be analysable by using other terms from the moral family—

---

[16] Moore, *Principia Ethica*.

'ought' or 'right', say. Is it simple? Well, that depends on what 'simple' means. If it means that some moral concept has to be taken as primitive, then there is no reason to object. But if it is taken to imply a peculiar metaphysics of concepts, where a simple concept is like some uniform sense-datum, then we might look upon the idea with justified suspicion (is goodness some particularly radiant patch of pure whiteness, perhaps?). As so often in philosophy, the truth turns out to be much less hypertrophic than we are inclined to suppose. The sense in which goodness is simple, unanalysable, and non-natural is pretty unexciting: it amounts to little more than the observation that we have a distinctive class of moral concepts at our disposal.

9. 'GOOD' AND 'OUGHT'

There remains one other source of moral psychologism that needs to be identified and punctured. This trades upon the conceptual connection between 'good' and 'ought'. As we have seen, it is constitutive of goodness that we ought to promote it: we ought to will the good. Thus there is an intrinsic connection between the concept of goodness and certain psychological concepts—those involved in the mental antecedents of action. The good is what we ought to *desire, intend, love*. In grasping the concept of goodness we appreciate its relation to our decision-making faculty. This point is sometimes taken to support psychologism, for it asserts a direct link between goodness and motivation.[17] When we judge that something is good, we are necessarily motivated to promote it—so the claim goes. But how can this be unless goodness is somehow reducible to desire or some other motivational mental state? Only desire or the like can dispose to action; goodness disposes to action; so goodness is a form of motivational state (or utterances of 'good' are expressions of desire or whatever). Moral talk must somehow be talk about psychological inclinations in order to explain how morality is intrinsically motivating.

[17] On the general issue, see Bernard Williams, 'Internal and External Reasons'. The idea that goodness is intrinsically motivating, and hence psychological in nature, is very widely endorsed—despite differences in the sort of psychological state thought to be required (belief or desire, say).

Much has been written about this kind of argument, but the point I want to make concerns the proper interpretation of the link between goodness and motivation—however motivation is understood. For that link can be taken in two ways that should not be confused. The first way is purely logical: it says that we *ought* to promote the good, whether or not anyone is actually inclined to do so. The second way is purely empirical: it says that as a matter of *fact* people are inclined to promote the good. Obviously these are totally distinct claims; neither entails the other. This means that there is no argument from the truth of the first claim to the conclusion that goodness is what people desire. You cannot derive an 'is' from an 'ought'. Goodness is indeed what is desir*able*, but there is no sound step from this to the thesis that the good is what is desir*ed*. There is clearly no *contradiction* in saying that what is morally desirable is universally shunned, since the notion of desirability is just the notion of what ought to be. The principle that we ought to will the good is actually not an empirical psychological claim of any kind. We must beware of psychologizing something that is not inherently a psychological matter.

The case is analogous to the notion of logical validity. If p entails q, then you ought to infer q from p: statements of logical consequence imply statements about how people ought to reason. But it would be a *non sequitur* to infer from *this* that the notion of logical consequence is somehow a psychological notion. Statements about how people *should* reason are not statements about how people *do* reason. The link between entailment and reasoning is normative, not descriptive. So it is with goodness and motivation: that we ought to be motivated in certain ways, given that certain things are good, is a normative principle, not a prediction about actual human psychology. So the uncontroversial point that moral properties are logically connected to ought-statements does not imply that moral properties are in any way mental. When I judge that something is good I do indeed know that I ought to act in certain ways, but whether I am disposed to act in those ways is another matter. And only the latter affords any support for psychologism.

Psychologism in logic has long been out of favour. But psychologism about moral properties seems to have a more tenacious hold. If what I have said in this chapter is right, however, moral psychologism should go the way of logical psychologism, and for essentially the same reasons. Both confuse what ought to be the case, logically or morally, with what is the case, psychologically. Thoughts are indeed *used* in both areas, but they are not mentioned. When we think about goodness we are not thinking about our own thoughts; we are thinking about something of an essentially non-mental kind.

3

Knowledge of Goodness

1. ETHICAL KNOWLEDGE AND SCIENTIFIC KNOWLEDGE

The concept of knowledge is a polymorphous concept, covering a wide variety of subjects. Consider knowledge of geography, history, psychology, language, physics, logic, mathematics, ethics. The methods used to acquire knowledge of these types are highly variable and the kinds of things known about differ radically. The underlying psychological capacities surely reflect these deep divisions. Our epistemic capacities have a modular organization.

Philosophers often try to bring order to this variety by classifying the different knowledge-systems in various ways. Thus we have the traditional great division between a priori and a posteriori knowledge, as well as the distinction between theoretical and practical knowledge, and between explicit and implicit knowledge, and no doubt others. There is a standing temptation to treat one or more varieties of knowledge as paradigmatic, so that the others must approximate to the paradigm if they are to earn the epithet 'knowledge'. Whole philosophies are erected on the basis of such a choice of paradigm. Empiricism is such a philosophy: explicit theoretical knowledge derived from experience is the favoured model of cognition. And it is a short step from this to the belief that *science* is the paradigm of knowledge. Given that 'knowledge' is an honorific term, it is just one further step to the conclusion that scientific knowledge has the greatest intrinsic value—that all other varieties of so-called knowledge are inferior to scientific knowledge.

But we should be wary of these tendencies to select one sort of knowledge as setting the standard for all the rest: this is apt to be arbitrary and tendentious, not founded upon the application of

3. SCIENCE AND INDUCTION

We can begin our critique of the above argument by noting that not all scientific facts impinge directly on our beliefs; our beliefs are largely mediated by *inference*. The data combine with our inferential rules to produce beliefs about facts that go beyond observation. The facts in which we believe seldom impinge themselves; rather, evidence and inference yield belief in these facts. So there is not the kind of simple control of belief by fact that the argument, as presented, assumes. Scientific belief is notoriously subject to the underdetermination of theory by data. Consider our beliefs in the truth of Darwinian theory or quantum theory: it is not that the truth of these theories guides our belief in them in any simple way; it does so only in a highly mediated way. And it is precisely because of this that science has the epistemic characteristics it has: the gap between data and hypotheses, and the reliance on non-deductive rules of inference. Much of science is, in a word, conjectural. This is why there is a real question as to whether our beliefs are being guided by the truth itself, as opposed to what our data and inferential practices tell us. Science is thus open to scepticism, as are our ordinary beliefs about the empirical world.

This is a familiar and indeed truistic point, but it is a point that needs to be reckoned with in the present context. Science is apt to be speculative; it is not in general some kind of simple registration of the objective facts. And there is a very specific reason for this: the reliance on induction and abduction as ways of going beyond the data. All knowledge of law and theory is based upon these two modes of inference. These guide belief formation as much as the causally operative objective facts. And it is because of their indispensable role that scepticism about scientific knowledge is so easy to formulate and fret over. We can only guarantee such knowledge if we can show these to be rules of inference that succeed in tracking the truth. But the plain fact is that we have no generally accepted solution to the problem of induction or the parallel problem of abduction (isn't it just a kind of *guessing*?). These principles are essential to science if it is to move any distance from simple observation, but their epistemic status remains problematic. There have been thinkers, indeed, who are so troubled by this that they adopt a kind of non-cognitivism about science: theoretical statements are not really true or false, but rather are merely useful instruments for the prediction of observations.[3] It is not that I agree with this extreme response to the epistemological travails of science; my point is just that such a position is by no means irrational or unmotivated. There really are substantive epistemological problems that scientific belief must face. How do we really *know* that we are tracking the objective truth, given that all we have to go on are limited data and rules of inference that look more like articles of faith than established certainties? The great prestige of science should not blind us to the very real epistemological concerns it raises—concerns that were quite apparent to philosophers of science during its infancy. These concerns may not trouble the practising scientist, but philosophical reflection on science cannot help but raise them. Nor need we embrace the kind of radical critique of science of some recent thinkers in order to acknowledge that science is not epistemologically invulnerable.[4]

But now we can notice a crucial distinction between ethical belief and scientific belief: ethical knowledge does not rely upon induction or abduction. It is therefore not prey to the epistemological anxieties those principles provoke. We believe it to be a law that bodies accelerate uniformly as they fall to earth on the basis of induction from past confirming instances, but we do not believe the 'law' that stealing is wrong by observing past confirming instances and then projecting to the future. For we do not *need* to rely on any such induction in the ethical case; we know that stealing is wrong just by knowing what stealing is. As Bertrand Russell once pointed out, here we have a species of noninductive knowledge of a universal statement, analogous to our knowledge of the universal truths of arithmetic, which are also not based on induction from positive instances.[5] Just as we do not need to observe several instances in which two things plus two things equal four things in order to know that two plus two

[3] This was the view of many logical positivists—that the theoretical sentences of physics, say, are not 'fact-stating'. One sometimes hears the same said today about the statements of folk psychology. Those who adopt such a view of moral statements do well to remember the company they keep.
[4] I mean the idea, traceable mainly to Thomas Kuhn's *The Structure of Scientific Revolutions*, that science is little more than a projection of sociology (to put it crudely). Of course, I utterly reject such a position.
[5] Bertrand Russell, *The Problems of Philosophy*, ch. 7.

equals four, so we do not need to examine a number of instances of stealing in order to confirm the generalization that stealing is always wrong. Thus, while it could turn out that the next observed swan is black, it *cannot* turn out that the next couple added to itself gives five, or that the next theft is morally splendid. We are dealing here with necessary truths known independently of inductive inference. And given that induction is epistemologically problematic, ethical knowledge is free of this problem.

This is a point that would I think be widely granted, but its significance is underappreciated. Because of it, the well-founded philosophical scepticism that attends scientific belief simply has no counterpart for ethical belief. We *hope* that our scientific beliefs reflect the facts, but this hope depends upon the justifiability of induction and abduction; in the case of ethics, however, we do not need to be troubled by this source of potential error. In this respect, then, ethical knowledge is superior to scientific knowledge.

4. ETHICS AND MATHEMATICS

The point I have just made is that moral knowledge is not based on inference to the best explanation, as scientific knowledge is, but this is turned to the advantage of moral knowledge. This does not, however, overturn the observation that ethical facts cannot in principle causally explain our belief in them. But is this a good objection to the idea of ethical knowledge? I think the asymmetry should be conceded, though there is room for quibbling in view of the causal chaos that surrounds quantum theory (the world may not be as well-behaved causally as we tend to think). But is it really a count against ethics that its subject-matter is causally inert? Does this show that ethical knowledge is not possible? Well, only if the same is true of logic and mathematics; for they, too, are not causally responsible for our knowledge of them.[6] But if the argument merely shows that ethics is epistemologically on a par with logic and mathematics, that is hardly to the detriment of ethics, since these are areas of knowledge in

---

[6] See Paul Benacerraf, 'Mathematical Truth'.

good standing, to put it mildly. All we have seen is that ethics belongs in a separate epistemological category from knowledge of the empirical world—which is not something that ought to surprise us.

John Locke explicitly remarks on the resemblance between ethics and mathematics, and locates the point within his broader epistemology. He says: 'Upon this ground it is, that I am bold to think, that *Morality is capable of Demonstration*, as well as Mathematicks: Since the precise real Essence of the Things moral Words stand for, may be perfectly known; and so the Congruity, or Incongruity of the Things themselves, be certainly discovered, in which consists perfect Knowledge.'[7] And again: 'I doubt not, but if a right method were taken, a great part of Morality might be made out with that clearness, that could leave, to a considering Man, no more reason to doubt, than he could have to doubt of the Truth of Propositions in Mathematicks, which have been demonstrated to him.'[8] This means, for Locke, that morality has the kind of epistemic accessibility that suits it to our natural capacities, that we 'may conclude, that *Morality* is *the proper Science, and Business of Mankind in general*'.[9] Because moral properties are transparent to us, unlike empirical natural kinds, we can come to firmer knowledge about them than we can in the empirical sciences, and we can do so without acquiring special expertise. Scientific knowledge is conjectural and inherently stretches our natural capacities, but moral knowledge has certainty and universality, and hence admits of demonstration. Locke clearly believes, then, that ethics has the epistemological advantages of mathematics, precisely because it does not deal with causally active natural kinds that we must know about only through interactions with our senses.

Russell made much the same point when he wrote:

A priori knowledge is not all of the logical kind we have been hitherto considering. Perhaps the most important example of non-logical *a priori* knowledge is knowledge as to ethical value. I am not speaking of judgements as to what is useful or as to what is virtuous, for such judgements do require empirical premises; I am speaking of judgements as to the

---

[7] Locke, *Essay Concerning Human Understanding*, 516.
[8] Ibid., 664.
[9] Ibid., 646.

intrinsic desirability of things . . . We judge, for example, that happiness is more desirable than misery, knowledge than ignorance, goodwill than hatred, and so on. Such judgements must, in part at least, be immediate and *a priori*. Like our previous *a priori* judgements, they may be *elicited* by experience, and indeed they must be; for it seems not possible to judge whether anything is intrinsically valuable unless we have experienced something of the same kind. But it is fairly obvious that they cannot be *proved* by experience; for the fact that a thing exists or does not exist cannot prove either that it is good that it should exist or that it is bad. The pursuit of this subject belongs to ethics, where the impossibility of deducing what ought to be from what is has to be established. In the present connexion, it is only important to realise that knowledge as to what is intrinsically of value is *a priori* in the same sense in which logic is *a priori*, namely in the sense that the truth of such knowledge can be neither proved nor disproved by experience.'[10]

Thus Russell responds to the non-empirical character of ethical knowledge, not by questioning the cognitive status of ethics, but by classifying such knowledge as a priori. And this seems to me exactly the right response: it is only dogmatic empiricism that allows us to repudiate any area of apparent knowledge simply because it does not conform to the perceptual paradigm. Ethics is simply one area among others in which empiricist epistemology breaks down.

In the light of the analogy between ethics and mathematics, it begins to look like blatant scientism to berate ethics for failing to mirror empirical scientific knowledge. Science is taken to set the standard not because it satisfies some impartial criterion of epistemic worth, but simply because it is science. Degree of certainty is a much less tendentious criterion, but ethics wins by that test, as noted above. So far, then, nothing has been said to undermine the credibility of ethics.

I suspect that lurking behind the appeal of the causal argument is a tacit adherence to the 'myth of the given'. We are prone to think that authentic knowledge should consist in a kind of bare confrontation between mind and fact, with the fact imprinting itself on the mind. The mind is conceived as a *tabula rasa* that receives the incoming fact without mediation. Then there is no distortion from the internal make-up of the knower. If the notion of being guided by the facts is construed in this way, then any-

[10] Russell, *The Problems of Philosophy*, 42–3.

thing that may be made to seem to conform to it will strike us as an especially meritorious kind of belief formation. And if ethical belief fails to fit this model, then it will seem to lack all objectivity.

But surely this picture is naïve in the extreme. The mind is a highly structured cognitive system. Knowledge is a coincidence between the way the mind is intrinsically constituted, innately and otherwise, and an independent reality.[11] So even in doing science we are not featureless subjects passively registering the external facts. But then the supposed contrast with ethics ought to seem less sharp: in both cases there is a non-trivial component to belief formation that comes from us. It is not that in science belief formation is 'all world', while in ethics it is 'all mind'; rather, this whole way of looking at things is based on a naïve view of the cognizing subject. In so far as the causal argument is nourished by such a picture, it is based upon faulty assumptions.

Should we conclude that there is *no* sense in which ethical truth can explain ethical knowledge? Granted, goodness does not causally explain our beliefs about it, but might there nevertheless be true 'because'-statements of some sort that link truth and belief? If so, we would be able to exhibit ethical beliefs as *sensitive* to the truth, which is what we expect of genuine knowledge. I think there is actually no obstacle to this. All that is required is that ethical beliefs *track* the truth in the sense that they are counterfactually dependent upon it. The truth of a proposition needs simply to be a reason for believing that a given subject believes that proposition. And this will be so just in case the subject is *reliable* with respect to propositions of that type—that is, given that he can distinguish truth from falsity with respect to that class of propositions.[12] Suppose I believe an arithmetical proposition if and only if it is true, while you believe such propositions according to whether they have a nice poetic ring to them, thus believing many arithmetical falsehoods. Then my beliefs can be predicted from the truth-value of the proposition, while yours

[11] For an elaboration of this perspective, see Noam Chomsky, *Language and Problems of Knowledge*, ch. 5.

[12] On knowledge as a discriminative capacity, see McGinn, 'The Concept of Knowledge'. I might note that there is no difficulty in producing Gettier cases for ethical knowledge (which I leave as an exercise for the interested reader), thus suggesting that the *concept* of knowledge works in the usual way when applied to the ethical domain. The contention that we cannot be properly said to *know* ethical propositions flies full in the face of our usual conceptual practices.

teaching; and we can accept that there are variations from group to group in ethical skills and judgements: but the basic structure is common and innately based. As Reid suggests, this type of knowledge is not like specialized technical knowledge that only certain individuals can acquire, as with the sciences; rather, like language, it is something that all humans are equipped to grasp, short of mental pathology. So there is a sense in which ethical knowledge is more solidly founded in our natural constitution than knowledge of science: we acquire it with less effort of will and mental labour, as we acquire language. Like language, too, it is so integral to human nature that we hardly notice its pervasiveness in our thinking and feeling. Science is apt to be at the forefront of conscious concentration, precisely because it is not part of universal human endowment; but language and ethics belong to the unreflective implicit area of the mind. That is why it is so hard to develop articulate theories of them: we have grammatical and ethical 'intuitions', but we are hard pressed to discover what the underlying principles are.

This way of looking at ethical competence bears on the observation, frequently made, that we have achieved striking progress in science, while in ethics our progress, such as it is, has been relatively unimpressive. Compare our physics to the physics of the Greeks, and our ethics with theirs. This may prompt some to claim an inferiority in ethics—since surely progress is a mark of epistemic merit. If ethics is a cognitive domain, shouldn't it display a steady increase of knowledge? The answer to this is obvious once the language analogy has been taken to heart. First, we should not underestimate the amount of moral progress that has been made in human history: it is not that we are permanently sunk in moral stagnation and error. Similarly, there has been linguistic progress, as the resources of language have expanded and been adapted to various literary and scientific purposes. And in areas in which moral progress has not been as great as one might wish, this is often because of powerful forces of greed and self-interest, not because the moral faculty is inherently sluggish. But the more important point, from a theoretical point of view, is that a history of progress may simply mark the poverty of the starting-point, rather than signalling the splendour of the end-point. If you start off in a state of extreme ignorance and incompetence, then you are likely to make rapid and impressive improvements;

while if you are well-endowed to begin with, there is not so far to go in terms of cognitive amelioration. Even the Greeks were remarkably bad at science by contemporary standards; yet Greek ethics was in many respects in a highly developed and sophisticated state—so much so that modern thinkers still advocate returning to its insights. This is just what you would expect if the Reid–Chomsky conception of ethical knowledge is correct: since we are innately predisposed to grasp ethical principles, we do not need to discover them laboriously over many centuries of trial and error, extensive observation, and ingenious theory construction. The case is just like language: how much progress has been made in speakers' knowledge of the fundamental principles of language? Is the basic linguistic competence of the ordinary speaker any greater now than at the time of the Greeks? Obviously not, because the innate basis of our linguistic knowledge has been fixed and hard-wired from then to now. Maybe during early hominid history rapid progress was made in using language from rudimentary beginnings. But by some thousands of years ago the language faculty had reached a steady state and no further improvements took place. Why should they?

Similarly for competence in folk psychology, which has stayed much the same too. This also is plausibly seen as an innate subsystem of human cognition. Its relative stability reflects this. The lack of 'progress' here is not a reason to think that knowledge of folk psychology is somehow suspect. What the constancy of these cognitive systems shows is not that they are discreditably stagnant, like some 'research programme' built on regressive foundations; rather, it shows that they simply do not have very far to go any more. They fulfil their purposes well enough; the basic principles are adequately represented. How much progress has been made in elementary arithmetic over the last two thousand years? None—because that was got right long ago. So, we do make *some* moral progress, perhaps by becoming more explicit about what we have already implicitly internalized; but the relative constancy of our moral judgements, at least at the level of basic principles, is no reason to doubt that we have here a case of genuine knowledge.

The linguistic model also provides a useful way to think about the phenomenon of moral disagreement or divergence. The languages of different cultures and epochs exhibit considerable surface dissimilarities, and the language of one group can seem entirely alien to another. But this is compatible with deep commonalities across superficially different languages—with the existence of linguistic universals. Much apparent ethical divergence surely has the same structure: a common fund of principles expressed and applied differently according to the contingencies of the environment—social, physical, and intellectual. Suppose for a moment that utilitarianism is true: aren't there indefinitely many ways in which the principle of maximizing the happiness of the greatest number might be expressed, depending upon what else is true of the society in question (for example, their religious beliefs about the afterlife)? My guess is that an enormous amount of so-called ethical disagreement reflects differences of application rather than adherence to radically opposing basic principles or dispositions.

But what of the supposed residue of disagreements that cannot be explained in that way? What does the alleged intractability of such disagreements show? Are they more irresoluble than other sorts of fundamental disagreement in science or philosophy? It seems to me that deep ethical disagreement is no more a reason to doubt the cognitive status of ethics than deep philosophical disagreement is a reason to doubt the cognitive status of philosophy, and basic disagreements in science (say in quantum theory) are apt to be philosophical in character. Indeed, fundamental disagreements in ethics tend to *be* philosophical disagreements. All that is shown by such disagreements is that when a framework of thought is questioned there is no secure place to go from which to resolve the disagreement. What is certainly not shown is that there is no fact of the matter as to who is right— crude verificationism is no more acceptable in ethics than elsewhere.

There is in fact a huge amount of basic agreement between cultures and epochs about simple morality, say about promise-keeping; more so than agreement in scientific or cosmological beliefs. And ethical disagreement is certainly responsive to rational persuasion. (I myself underwent a radical change of moral outlook with respect to animals some twenty-five years ago, and I flatter myself that it was rationally driven.) Such disagreement as there is does not indicate some total relativism in what people morally believe. And the fact that some people might accept some pretty wild moral ideas no more undermines the authority of what most people accept than the fact that some people still hold some pretty wild scientific beliefs undermines accepted science. All sorts of factors can explain such disagreements, and I see no more reason to think this is to the discredit of ethics than it is to the discredit of science or philosophy or history. Indeed, the fact that people *disagree*, rather than just express different preferences, already shows that they take there to be some truth over which they are contending. Disagreement can only threaten the cognitive status of ethics if there is no such thing as genuine disagreement. Anyway, the plain fact is that there are many things that are obviously morally wrong—murder, torture, theft, betrayal—and anyone who disagrees about these is either dishonest or confused. That is simply part of common sense, and no reason has been produced to deny it. Short of radical scepticism, these judgements are as solid as any we make.

I strongly suspect that sociologists and anthropologists have grossly exaggerated the variations in the moral attitudes of different societies, partly out of misguided philosophical relativism, but also in order to confer greater interest on the practice of those disciplines; for they would hardly seem as full of fascinating surprises if all cultures actually converged in their basic views of life. In the same way the study of alien languages loses some of its interest if all languages turn out to share a basic structure. The human mind is much like the human body in this respect: human bodies clearly differ in all sorts of ways, but it would be an obvious mistake to conclude that there is no fundamental convergence of physiological type in the human species—as a comparison with the bodies of animals of other species shows. Maybe if we encountered Martians who really did differ morally from us (and were quite wrong in their values—holding, say, that stealing is wrong only if you don't murder the person you steal from), then we would see more clearly how much we humans really do agree morally. There is such a thing as cognitive human nature, as our shared biology suggests; and it seems only reasonable to expect that our moral sense, like our linguistic capacities, will reflect that common nature.

6. TRUTH AND COERCION

According to the (or one) pragmatic theory of truth, the truth of a belief consists in its utility and the falsity of a belief consists in its disutility. If you believe what is true, you will succeed in negotiating the world successfully; if you believe what is false, the world will make you pay. Truth is not neutral with respect to the believer's utilities, since belief interacts with desire to produce action. There is a sense in which the world *forces* truth upon us by impeding or aiding our projects. Suppose you were to believe completely false things about the physical world—about gravity, electricity, arsenic, or whatever. Then you would soon find yourself in grave physical trouble—dead, ultimately. The world would, so to speak, inform you of your errors; it would act to correct them. Let us put this by saying that truth and falsity are *coercive*. We are not free to believe whatever we like about nature, not if we want to thrive. Hence the appeal of the pragmatic theory.

But in ethics, error does not have this kind of penalty and truth this kind of reward. The moral facts will not step in to correct my mistakes, coercing me to believe in them. The reason for this is simply that moral facts do not have causal powers. If I believe that gravity has the power to hold me aloft as I step from a high building, then its actual causal powers will soon teach me otherwise. But if I believe that murder is right, then nothing about its wrongness will *cause* me to recognize my error. Moral truth is non-coercive. Of course, I may well suffer practical penalties from other people, but the moral facts themselves will do nothing to harm me. The point here is not the earlier one that moral facts do not causally explain my beliefs; the point is rather that they do not act to thwart or satisfy my desires. I won't fall on my head by having false moral beliefs, thus thwarting my desire to have an intact head. The world does not operate to keep my moral beliefs in line, to impose cognitive discipline on me. In this sense, then, I *am* free to believe what I like morally.

So there is an important epistemological asymmetry between natural belief and ethical belief—that truth is coercive in the one case but not in the other. But this is not a reason to suppose that the idea of ethical truth is chimerical; it just shows a difference in the way truth in the two cases connects with our utilities. What it does tell us, however, is something important about the motivation for having true beliefs in the ethical case. In the case of natural or scientific belief, we have a reason to pursue the truth independently of the value of truth itself, namely that it aids our desire satisfaction. But in ethics this motivation is lacking, since ethical truth has no pay-off and error no penalty. And this means that there is a real question here about why I *should* seek ethical truth. In the case of natural belief, this question can be answered, but in the ethical case there is no answer—save that we ought to believe what is true *for its own sake*. In other words, ethical truth is a value that lacks pragmatic justification.

It is not that I find this intolerable; my point is that it shows something distinctive about the nature of morality and our relation to it. Since ethical truth is essentially non-coercive, we *must* pursue it for its own sake. There is a purity about our motivation for achieving ethical truth that is not found in the case of natural belief. To put it differently: the search for moral truth has no prudential justification, as the search for scientific truth does (at least in principle). In trying to arrive at ethical truth we are not guided by the world's impact on our state of well-being. We are guided by value in somewhat the way we are guided by rules—normatively, not as a matter of brute force. We might even say that the terrible thing about goodness is that it is powerless to impose the truth about itself on us; we must *choose* to accept its dictates, because it cannot rear up and bite us for rejecting it. Gravity, by contrast, can rely on its own nature to persuade us to believe the truth about it and act accordingly. There is, to echo a theme of the existentialists, a kind of radical freedom involved in accepting values, which there is not for beliefs about the empirical world. This freedom does not mean that anything goes; it means merely that values cannot coerce us into accepting them. My suspicion is that a lot of the relativism and scepticism about morality that we see has its conceptual source in this point. Perhaps once it has been properly articulated it can be seen for what it is—a genuinely distinctive feature of morality but not one that threatens its cognitive status. Only crude prudential pragmatism could do that, combined with the non-coercive character of ethical truth.

Intellectual virtue in science and ethics differs as a consequence. In science the intellectual virtue of pursuing the truth has a kind of prudential backing, at least in the large: if our beliefs are false, we are apt to suffer as a result. But in ethics intellectual virtue has no such prudential backing—it must be its own justification. This means that in ethics you have to be virtuous to be a believer in the good, while in science you can pursue the truth with no more virtue than enlightened self-interest. Greater moral credit therefore attaches to true moral belief than to true scientific belief, as a matter of conceptual necessity. This result seems to me to be confirmed by our intuitions.

Perhaps it is partly a reluctance to accept that ethical reality is non-coercive that prompts the idea that ethical truths are like commands of some sort. In the case of commands, there is a coercive element present because non-compliance typically carries a sanction, imposed by the authority that issues the command. If ethical principles were really commands, then they would, by their very logic, carry rewards and penalties. This would restore some parity to the case of natural beliefs, though now the coercion goes via the agency of another. Indeed, the idea that moral utterances are commands can only be justified if the coercive element is present—otherwise the idea is empty. This may serve to remove the fear that ethics is a sanction-free area in which any kind of belief is as kindly treated by reality as any other. Ethical sentences say 'Do so and so, *or else!*', and that last bit is what provides the element of coercion.

But of course this is all quite mistaken: there is no authority backing ethical requirements that will impose sanctions on moral deviation. That is, their prescriptive power does not intrinsically depend upon the existence of any such authority (even if God exists he does not *create* ethical requirements). Ethical statements are precisely unlike commands in this respect. What is sometimes called the 'moral law' is not any kind of *law*, properly speaking, since ethical norms are not necessarily backed by a penal system of some sort. There simply is no central authority that will step in to enforce moral compliance. And even if there were, as a matter of contingent fact, that is not what the 'authority' of morality depends upon: it depends simply upon what is good or bad, right or wrong—in themselves. A command, by contrast, derives its authority from the power structure that surrounds it, and this really is a matter of what the world will do to you if you disobey. But moral 'disobedience' is not like that: it consists simply in doing what is wrong. We find this a disturbing idea, no doubt, which is why the command model can seem attractive, either as literal theory or as metaphor. But it is actually part of the very essence of morality that its prescriptions be non-coercive. There is no 'or else!' in morality, not considered in itself. What I know when I know that something is right is not that I have to do it or else I will be punished, but rather simply that I *ought* to do it, for no other reason than that. Moral principles are indeed *directive* in the sense that they tell us what we ought to do, but that is not at all the same thing as to say they are of the nature of commands. It is precisely because moral utterances are *not* commands that acceptance of them is as prudentially motiveless as it is.

It is worth noting explicitly that the non-coerciveness of ethical truth is at odds with any view that identifies goodness with a psychological property (or any other natural property). I have already rejected this idea in the previous chapter, but now we can observe that if such a reductive thesis were true then there *would* be a form of worldly coercion in ethics. Suppose we identify being good with being desired by people; then to deny that something is good would be to deny that people desire it. But now suppose that I falsely deny that something is good: that means that I deny that people desire it when they do in fact desire it. But that will bring me into conflict with the psychological facts, and they have real causal potency in the world. I will act as if people don't desire something they do desire, and this will put me at risk of their displeasure. The world will likely step in to correct my false belief. But that means that my false belief that the thing in question was not good will be corrected by the fact that it is good, since goodness is what is desired. Moral error will have its costs if goodness is some kind of natural property. Equivalently, there will be a prudential motive to be moral. But I think it is obvious that this gives the wrong account of moral error—we do not see it as corrigible in such ways. We cannot rely on the natural world to shape our moral beliefs in the direction of the truth.

This point is apt to be obscured by the way the moral supervenes on the natural. It is true that beliefs about the natural properties that moral properties supervene upon are open to the impact of the facts in the usual way. And it is also true that these beliefs may function as premises in an inference to the moral quality of a situation. Thus I may judge that a situation is good because I believe that it contains a lot of pleasure, and that belief is open to coercion by the facts, since pleasure has causal powers. One might then think that the moral belief ought to be equally corrigible, since it must be true if the belief about pleasure is true (by supervenience). But really this is a *non sequitur*: once I move to the moral plane I step outside the causal realm and my error will not be corrigible by the moral fact itself—not, that is, by anything other than the mere moral truth of the matter. If I judge of what is really pleasure that it is pleasure and that it is bad, then my moral mistake will not be exposed by what the object of my error does in response. The fact that pleasure actually has the property of goodness will not itself visit any rude awakening upon me. It is true that if I act to decrease the pleasure in the mistaken belief that it is bad, then the object of my action will offer resistance; but this is because of the decrease of pleasure, not because I believe, mistakenly, that pleasure is bad. If I judge of two naturalistically indistinguishable situations that one is good and the other bad, then I am liable to find myself corrected by the facts as I act differentially towards them; but that will be because of the naturalistic facts themselves, not the moral facts that I have got wrong. It will never be in virtue of the moral facts that the world causes a change in my beliefs.

So we can say that moral facts are strongly dependent on facts that are coercive in the intended sense, but that they are not themselves coercive. Here we see what is perhaps the distinguishing mark of value: values supervene on the causal without themselves being causal.[16] Thus there can be no moral difference between situations without there being a causal difference, but moral distinctions themselves *make* no causal difference. Moral properties are at the same time causally epiphenomenal and yet strongly constrained by the causal. Supervenient natural properties, such as psychological properties, are themselves causal; only values appear to combine non-causality and supervenience on the causal. This is because they are evaluative in their essence: they are required to be responsive to the natural facts, since this is what they evaluate—hence supervenience; yet they must also be non-causal, since this follows directly from their evaluative na-

[16] Cf. Moore, 'The Conception of Intrinsic Value'. Moore even takes this, tentatively, as a *definition* of value.

ture (as I argued in the previous chapter). So it is built into values that they should combine the two features. If this is right, then we can define the evaluative as what is both supervenient on the causal and yet non-causal. This won't yet quite define *moral* value, since other evaluative concepts seem to combine the two features as well—such as aesthetic and logical evaluations. To single out the moral values, we cannot do better than to use the notion of the moral directly—they are the values that are of concern to *morality*. But still this definition does give us some sort of external handle on what being evaluative looks like from a metaphysical point of view. Values are what the causal realm determines without themselves being causal.

We can now say, putting the two points together, that it is the evaluative aspect of moral properties which makes them non-coercive, since it is what underlies their non-causality. It is because goodness tells us what we ought to do that it cannot correct us for not doing it. The evaluative nature of moral properties is what makes them irrelevant to desire satisfaction. So three essential elements of moral reality hang together: its evaluativeness, its non-causality, and its pragmatic pointlessness (there being nothing that forces its truth on us). This last epistemological feature is thus connected internally to the ontology of the properties in question. I ought to desire your welfare, but my moral belief that your welfare is good is not a belief whose truth will result in *my* welfare being enhanced, since moral properties, being evaluative, are causally inert. We can thus deduce that morality cannot be prudentially motivated in the way natural science can be, from the very fact that its key concepts are essentially evaluative.

7. MORALITY AND FOLK PSYCHOLOGY

I have suggested that the moral faculty has an innate basis. But this raises the question: why should morality be innate in the mind? What is it doing there? What is the natural history of the moral faculty? We should not assume, in answering this, that the moral sense must have a clear biological function just because it is part of our innate endowment, since many innate characteristics have no direct biological advantage. This is typically because they are by-products of something else that does have a function. Such by-products can even be disadvantageous to the organism, but they persist because of the advantage conferred by what they are by-products of. So, even if ethics is counter to our biological fitness, that is not in itself a reason to doubt its innateness. What we have to ask is what it might derive from that *does* have a demonstrable advantage.

A plausible suggestion is that it is a by-product of our innate grasp of folk psychology. There is good reason to believe that this is innate, like language, and it is has a fairly clear biological function—to enable the organism to cope better with other psychological beings in a social environment. Equipped with an implicit grasp of belief-desire psychology, we can explain and predict the behaviour of others with considerable success. And this is something the infant needs to have in place sooner rather than later. Good biological design would imprint it on the genes. But now we can note that ethics is deeply embedded in folk psychology; the two systems interact at every point. Obligation presupposes belief, desire, and intention; praise and blame presuppose free will; the concept of well-being presupposes pleasure and pain. There could be no such thing as a mastery of moral concepts that did not involve a mastery of psychological concepts. But by the same token it is hard to see how a mastery of folk psychology, including the concept of the objective existence of distinct persons, could fail to lead naturally to a grasp of moral categories. Not indeed by logical deduction, but by virtue of 'general intelligence'. Once you have the concept of pain, and you have general reflective intelligence, then you are virtually bound to see that it is a bad thing—for others as well as yourself. The case is similar to our knowledge of natural science: once you have the basic concepts of common-sense physics, and enough general intelligence, you will be able to develop a scientific understanding of the world as a by-product. Of course, very little is known about how this works, but the general outlines seem plausible enough. The suggestion, then, is that ethical understanding arises naturally from the systematic deployment of psychological concepts—these being the concepts most centrally involved in moral evaluation. It is not that ethical concepts can be analysed in psychological terms; the suggestion is merely that the two sets of concepts are made for each other. After all, moral properties do supervene on psychological ones, substantially if not exclusively.[17]

If this is right, then we would expect two levels of moral thinking, corresponding to two levels of psychological thinking. There is the primitive, spontaneous level rooted in the innate schematism, and there is the mature, reflective level that comes when the primitive level is critically scrutinized. Philosophy of mind and decision theory attempt to formalize and articulate our intuitive psychological judgements; moral theory attempts to organize the moral reactions we spontaneously bring to the world. The two levels correspond to distinct cognitive faculties, and should not be conflated. In particular, difficulties at the reflective level should not be construed as inherent flaws in the primitive level. Much of mature moral life consists in trying to bring the two levels into alignment (compare the development of human sexuality).[18]

8. EPISTEMOLOGICAL QUEERNESS

It is often supposed that a cognitivist view of morality embroils us in insoluble epistemological problems. For how do our cognitive capacities relate to the supposed realm of ethical fact? How do those non-causal properties come to be apprehended by the knowing mind? Must we resort to an obscure notion of ethical intuition—a supersensory faculty that mysteriously locks onto transcendent realities? What becomes of naturalistic epistemology then? These are genuine questions, but I do not think their difficulty should deter us from accepting that we do have knowledge of ethical fact, for the following reasons.

[17] This by-product conception of moral knowledge might be compared with Chomsky's suggestion that arithmetical competence is a by-product of the language faculty: *Language and Problems of Knowledge*, 169–70, 183–4.

[18] This two-tier picture of ethical knowledge is analogous to the two-tier structure of linguistic knowledge. We know the rules of grammar implicitly, by virtue of our subconscious innate endowment; but we also have some explicit conscious knowledge of grammar, which linguists hope will one day recapitulate what is known implicitly. Similarly, there is the implicit knowledge contained *in* our 'moral module', on the one hand, and the explicit knowledge we try to formulate *about* that implicit knowledge, on the other. The incompleteness or shakiness of the reflective level of knowledge is not a reason to suppose that the implicit level is anything other than sure, reliable, and correct.

First, this is really just a special case of the problem of a priori knowledge, so ethics is in no worse case than logic and mathematics. It differs from them in involving knowledge of what *ought* to be so rather than just what *is* or *must* be so, since ethics has a distinctively evaluative subject-matter. But it is like them in not resting upon causal transactions and perceptual acquaintance by means of our sense-modalities. It is knowledge of *ideals,* in one sense—states of affairs that would obtain if the world were as it morally ought to be. When I grasp that something is logically necessary I grasp that it holds in all possible worlds; when I grasp that something ought to be I grasp that it holds in all morally desirable worlds: surely there is no surprise in the 'discovery' that such knowledge is not based on causal interactions, by means of the senses, with how the world actually is. Just as Kant taught us that experience can tell us only what *is* so, not what *must* be so, so experience cannot tell us what *ought* to be so. Knowledge, as I have remarked, is a polymorphous concept, so that we should not bewail the fact of its irreducible variety. Even within the category of the a priori, there are important subdivisions—as between knowledge of the evaluative and knowledge of the non-evaluative.

The general problem of the a priori is too large and digressive to take on now, but I can at least state my own position on it.[19] I hold that the nature of a priori knowledge involves questions that take us beyond the range of our intellectual powers, so that we are not going to understand the workings of the relevant faculties. This is not because those workings are ontologically queer or miraculous; it simply reflects our epistemic limitations. So ethical knowledge is indeed a mystery to us, but that is no reason to doubt its existence. Consciousness is also a mystery to us—the queer phenomenon *par excellence*—but we should not conclude that it does not exist.[20] We can know that something is so without understanding *how* it is so.

Actually, it is really not clear that we understand the processes involved in generating *any* kind of knowledge. There are no real

---

[19] This can be found in a more developed form in McGinn, *Problems in Philosophy,* ch. 6.

[20] I discuss the mysterious nature of consciousness in *The Problem of Consciousness.*

theories even of how we know about simple properties of the environment. The contributions of consciousness and abduction to knowledge-generation are steeped in mystery. We don't even understand how a stimulus produces a conscious percept in the mind. So it is not as if everything is plain sailing outside the category of the a priori. There are deep explanatory problems about ethical knowledge, but there are about all types of knowledge. This is not a reason to deny that we have knowledge and that it is perfectly robust and reliable.

There has been much debate about whether ethical knowledge should be characterized as 'perceptual' and 'intuitive'. I think neither description is happy, at least in natural senses of those terms. The moral faculty cannot be perceptual in any literal sense since there is no sense-organ devoted to ethical fact, and any sense-organ can be used to acquire factual information on which to base ethical judgements. Nor is there any sensory phenomenology associated with ethical 'intuitions'. The only serious respect in which ethical knowledge resembles perceptual knowledge is that it can be basic, that is, not arrived at by inference. But that does not warrant use of the word 'perception', any more than basic logical or mathematical knowledge can be so described.

What about 'intuition'? If we take the word in a stipulative sense just to mean 'not known by proof from something else and not perceptual', then there is no objection to its use. But it usually carries more colour than that, suggesting a form of super-reliable guessing or divining, analogous to religious revelation. Such an interpretation should be rejected, less because of its metaphysical presuppositions than because it is phenomenologically inaccurate. Our ethical 'intuitions' are much more like our 'intuitions' that certain strings of words are grammatical, as the analogy I drew earlier would suggest. They result from a kind of implicit mastery of a cognitive system that yields spontaneous verdicts. We can speak harmlessly of 'grammatical intuition', so long as we interpret the phrase correctly; and 'ethical intuition' is innocent too, taken in that way. The essential thrust of it is that we may not be able to articulate the general principles that underlie our particular judgements. What is unacceptable is to think of intuition on the model of a spirit medium contacting another supernatural world. No comparably eerie feeling accompanies our ethical intuitions.

Discussions of ethical knowledge are apt to take empiricism as the background position. Empirical knowledge is reckoned unproblematic and everything else is judged by this standard. My response to this has been twofold: in the first place, it rules out much more than ethical knowledge—logic, mathematics, modality, and so on; in the second, empirical knowledge is itself problematic. The very concept of experience harbours some of the deepest mysteries in philosophy—notably, how experience is possible in a physical world (the mind–body problem). So there is nothing uniquely perplexing about ethical knowledge.

Normally, then, we presume that there is ethical knowledge. People have it as a matter of course, and they are often quite certain of it. It is not based on induction and hypothesis formation. It comes naturally to us on the basis of our innate endowment. Thus it differs from scientific knowledge in certain respects, but not in any way that casts doubt on its status as knowledge. There is no good reason to doubt our common-sense conviction that we straightforwardly *know* that stealing is wrong. The property of goodness really is an object of human cognition.

4

The Evil Character

1. TWO TYPES OF MORAL PSYCHOLOGY

Imagine the following two species of beings—call them the G-beings and the E-beings. The G-beings are such that when another member of the species experiences pleasure they too experience pleasure, while when another experiences pain they feel pain. The interpersonal laws of feeling preserve pleasure and pain, so that cause and effect will be of the same hedonic type. The E-beings, on the other hand, exemplify the opposite laws of social psychology: pleasure in one causes pain in another, and pain causes pleasure. This, we can suppose, is just a matter of how they have been constructed biologically. If an E-being sees another stub his toe and yelp, she experiences a rush of pleasurable sensation, while if she sees someone enjoying a fresh melon, she feels a nasty sensation. These sensations of pleasure and pain could be anything from simple bodily pleasures and pains, like orgasm and toothache, to elevated states of emotion, like aesthetic rapture or deep despair. What matters is that the two species invert each other's interpersonal hedonic laws. Their hedonic dispositions are the exact reverse of each other.

Now, supposing that members of both species pursue their own pleasure, what will we expect of their behaviour? What will it take to maximize their respective utilities? The answer is obvious: the G-beings will promote and seek out pleasurable sensations in others, since this contributes to their own pleasure; while the E-beings will promote and seek out painful sensations in others, since—given the way they are hooked up—this will contribute to their pleasure. The more pain the E-beings can cause the more pleasure they will receive, and the more pleasure there is around them the more painful their life will be. Each will be out to maximize the pain of others as a way of maximizing his own pleasure. The G-beings, on the other hand, are out to maximize the pleasure of others, given their hedonic dispositions. (We can suppose, if we like, that neither species has any choice about enacting their given dispositions.) Thus, concretely, E-beings will be apt to become torturers, sadists, thieves, rapists, child abusers—whatever causes distress in others: the strong will exploit the weak, compassion will not exist, they will be continually at each other's throats. As I have described the case, however, they will not be murderers, since I did not stipulate that they derive pleasure from the *death* of others, considered in itself. We can include this if we like, but for the moment I want to consider a case without it. The G-beings, by contrast, will be kind, generous, compassionate, helpful, solicitous, brimming with fellow-feeling. Their desires will be uniformly altruistic, while those of their polar opposites will be cruel and malicious. And this is just what we would predict given the way their respective psychologies have been set up, pleasure being what it is.

This is an imaginary pair of species, but let me observe now that the E-beings are not entirely fanciful as a description of the ways of the animal kingdom. Given the received view of animal behaviour, there is ruthless competition between members of the same species (unless the genetic overlap is high, as with kin). The harm of conspecifics is generally speaking to the advantage of other competing members: if they are hungry, you are more likely not to be; if they have no mate, it is more likely that you do. Animals do not go around contributing to the well-being of other animals, unless there is something in it for them (or their genes). This is why apparently altruistic behaviour is a puzzle for evolutionary theory. So the hedonic dispositions of the E-beings are actually of a sort to be predicted by evolutionary theory. Of course, the human species is just one among many evolved species, and no exception to its basic laws (though these may be qualified in various ways).

But let us stick with our imaginary beings for the moment, so that the complexities of the real world can be kept at bay for a while. My point in introducing them is to provide a model for two types of moral psychology: that of the virtuous person, and that of the evil person. Focusing on the evil person, then, and simplifying for the moment, the basic idea is that an evil character is one that derives pleasure from pain and pain from pleasure.

I mean here to be discussing what we might call *pure* evil as opposed to *instrumental* evil—malice for its own sake, not as a means to achieving some other goal. I am not concerned with cases in which a person does something to harm another in order to reap some benefit, as with violent theft or fraud or some such: here the pain of the other is not the *goal* of the act, only a necessary (and perhaps regretted) means towards achieving something else. These are cases of immoral selfishness or egoism. I am concerned rather with cases in which the other's pain is prized for its own sake, in which the motive is precisely to cause suffering. This is not egoistic in the traditional sense, since no benefit to the agent accrues from the other's pain, aside from the pleasure afforded by it. We are to be concerned with cases in which my well-being is enhanced simply by the misery of others.

A standard example from fiction can be found in Herman Melville's *Billy Budd*,[1] a tale of stark malice clashing with naïve innocence. John Claggart is a naval master-at-arms who conceives a desire to harm and destroy Billy Budd, a lowly foretopman, on no further provocation than Billy's natural virtue and innocence. No advantage will accrue to Claggart from Billy's downfall; he wants it for its own sake. As the aged Dansker, to whom Billy goes for advice, pithily remarks: 'Baby Budd, *Jemmy Legs* [meaning the master-at-arms] is down on you.' (26)—not because of anything Billy has done, but simply and solely because of his natural virtue. There is, and there is meant to be, something inexplicable in the nature of Claggart's character: 'For what can more partake of the mysterious than an antipathy spontaneous and profound such as is evoked in certain exceptional mortals by the mere aspect of some other mortal, however harmless he may be, if not called forth by this very harmlessness itself?' (28). Claggart is said to have a temperament 'the direct reverse of a saint' (28) and to be suffering from a 'Natural Depravity: a depravity according to nature' (29). Though such a man's bearing 'would seem to intimate a mind peculiarly subject to the law of reason, not the less in heart he would seem to riot in complete exemption from that law, having apparently little to do

[1] Page references in the text are to the edition cited in the Bibliography. The story is helpfully discussed by Peter Kivy: 'Melville's *Billy*, and the Secular Problem of Evil: the Worm in the Bud.'

with reason further than to employ it as an ambidexter imple-
ment for effecting the irrational' (30). Claggart is a man 'in whom
was the mania of an evil nature, not engendered by vicious train-
ing or corrupting books or licentious living, but born with him
and innate' (30). The only motive he has in his campaign of destruction is that of envy of Billy's goodness. Indeed, we are told
that he is one of the few men aboard with the intellect and dis-
cernment to appreciate 'the moral phenomenon presented in
Billy Budd' (32). He is capable of 'apprehending the good, but
powerless to be it' (32). His character is so constituted that, despite his moral awareness, he cannot help but seek out the destruction of the Handsome Sailor. He is formed in such a way as
to hate virtue and to hate the pleasures of the virtuous. Claggart
is a man of few pleasures himself, save that of relishing Billy's
downfall and his own part in it. (The outcome is not, however, as
he anticipates: upon accusing Billy of mutinous intentions before
Captain Vere, Billy, unable to speak, strikes him a powerful blow
to the forehead, killing him stone dead. A just conclusion, we
may feel, but now the Captain must exact the required punish-
ment on Billy for striking an officer, namely death, all the while
knowing that Claggart had evilly plotted against him.)

What we need to take from this emblematic story is contained
in Melville's description of Claggart's temperament as the 'direct
reverse of a saint', for this neatly encapsulates the conception I
am working with—the idea of an inversion of the usual laws of
interpersonal feeling. Iago in Shakespeare's *Othello* might be
cited as another example of the type, though his psychology is
somewhat underdescribed. Envy is certainly a part of his motivation, and the envy is similar to Claggart's of Billy. Iago revealingly says of Cassio: 'He hath a daily beauty in his life that makes
me ugly' (v. i). The happiness and virtue of others is a sufficient
incitement to Iago's animosity. He must expunge the moral gap
between himself and others, eventually inciting Othello to murder. He revels in Othello's suffering and relishes the breakdown
of his character. The phenomenon in question, then, is that of the
malevolent motiveless action, or the character from which such
actions spring. We are not dealing here with your average rogue,
cheat, or traitor—someone with something to gain from his mis-
deeds. We are concerned with individuals with no other purpose
than that of harm and destruction—those who find pleasure in

the pain of others for its own sake. And the question is how such people are to be understood.

2. CLARIFYING THE ANALYSIS

It is a conceptual truth that evil requires distinctness of persons according to the present analysis of it: it involves *inter*personal psychological relations. The evil person derives pleasure precisely from someone *else*'s pain. On metaphysical views according to which there is only one self, no genuine evil will be possible. Sadism becomes mere masochism if I am not ontologically distinct from my victim. What matters to me is that it is someone else who is suffering, *not* me. Not only must the victim be distinct from the agent, the agent must be *aware* of the distinctness; indeed it is something he relishes. The evil intention has built into its very content the idea that the other is fully other. Anything that qualifies or weakens this otherness reduces the evil of the act; any conception that unifies agent and victim tends to undermine the possibility of evil. So a robust notion of personal identity is presupposed by the evil act—the idea of a firm boundary between oneself and others. It is no use my enjoying *my* pain in someone else's body if evil is what I intend; it has to be *his* pain that I enjoy—the pain of an autonomous subject of awareness.[2] Evil essentially requires perceived separateness of persons. For familiar reasons, this will depend upon my thinking of myself and others in indexically determined ways.[3] I could form the plan to make Colin McGinn suffer out of evil intentions by not realizing that I *am* Colin McGinn. I can do this only because I make the (false) judgement, 'I am not Colin McGinn.' So the evil person must form an intention whose content contains a concept like *him* or *you*, not one that corresponds simply to a proper name or definite description. I intend that *he* shall suffer. Merely causing suffering in *someone* isn't enough; it needs to be backed by this indexically based notion of a plurality of selves distinct from me.

---

[2] I am alluding here to section 302 of Wittgenstein's *Philosophical Investigations*, about the distinction between *your* feeling pain and *my* feeling pain in your body.

[3] See John Perry, 'The Essential Indexical'.

Psychologically, then, we would expect ideas of family and community to push against the evil impulse, while anything that suggests diversity and difference will reinforce it. Evil feeds off the notion of otherness. The pleasure of evil has the idea of the victim's sharp distinctness from me built into it: what I relish is that it is *not me* that is suffering. Anything that unites the victim with me will therefore cut against my ability to form evil intentions. It need hardly be noted, however, that the existence of a genuine plurality of selves is not seriously to be denied, so the evil agent is not likely to be deprived of the preconditions of his evil projects.

The notions of pleasure and pain must be taken broadly in the analysis; they are not restricted to bodily sensations. I think these are broad notions as we ordinarily understand them, and it is theoretically useful to employ them generously; so any kind of happiness or unhappiness, harm or enjoyment, should be included. Thus we can include the pleasure of conniving to prevent a rival scientist from receiving the prize that is her due, as well as deriving sexual pleasure from the bodily pain of others. Pleasure and pain are to be interpreted as correlative with attraction and aversion broadly construed.

The evil person can be either agent or spectator of the suffering he relishes. He need not always go to the trouble of bringing it about himself; he might be quite content if someone else, or just nature, does the harm. What matters is the state that pain produces in him, not necessarily his agency in producing it. Thus we might distinguish between active and passive evil, depending upon the agent's own intentional involvement.

We should note that the analysis includes pain in another's pleasure as well as pleasure in his pain. These are just two sides of the same coin, part of the same hedonic structure. The former is less often associated with evil, but only because it is less salient, not because it is not part of the psychology. There is no victim of this kind of evil, though there may soon become one as the evil agent tries to replace his pain by pleasure. To be distressed by the well-being of others is the first step towards wanting to remove that well-being, and is in any case a kind of malice (though perhaps of a less culpable sort).

The analysis as presented so far makes no mention of indifference as a form of evil—the idea that someone might be evil just because they do not care one way or the other about someone else's pain. This is certainly part of our ordinary understanding of evil, but it seems to me that it is sufficiently distinct from the kinds of case I am interested in that we can leave it aside. We could either think of it as a distinct species of evil—or moral failing, because 'evil' seems too strong—or we could simply add it as a disjunct to what we have so far. Then evil will be *either* taking pleasure in pain and pain in pleasure *or* being indifferent to pain (and indeed pleasure). In the case of indifference there is nothing in it for me in the pain of another; his pain simply fails to engage my hedonic dispositions. So I will not promote it or seek it out: it simply leaves me cold. It may be that such indifference is the end result of evil in the narrower sense, as when a person becomes sated with the pleasure of doing harm. The pleasure centres of the evil agent have become overstimulated and fatigued and what once caused exquisite delight (say, the slaughter of unbelievers) now leaves the spectator bored and apathetic. This indifferent person would be evil in the strict sense, but only because of her prior history of evil pleasure and pain. On the other hand, the 'indifference' of a rock or a cat to the pain of another hardly qualifies as a case of evil, even in the most attenuated sense. The case of the psychopath is intermediate: he has (we are told) lost the capacity to distinguish good from bad (so he is like the rock), but he also seems capable of terrible acts (so he is like the hedonistic sadist). It is difficult to know what to make of this kind of indifference; my own suspicion is that there is more active pleasure in it than is usually thought. Calm enjoyment can look a lot like complete indifference. Think of the sneer of disdain of the 'indifferent' man as he pointedly ignores the sufferings of others. Contempt of this kind has a large element of enjoyment in it.

The analysis has a straight counterexample as it stands: what if I am confronted by the pain felt by an evil person at the pleasure of another, or the pleasure he feels at the pain of another? Surely I should not feel pain at his pain and pleasure at his pleasure, since these are *evil* pleasures and pains. Clearly, there is no virtue in my being happy that the torturer is happy in his torturing. The way to get round this is simply to build in the condition that no link in the chain of causally connected hedonic states be one that inverts the pain-to-pain and pleasure-to-pleasure connections. There must be no evil kink in the chain. If there is one, then virtue requires an inversion to correct it. Perhaps, indeed, there are few things so distressing to the virtuous person than the palpable pleasure felt by the evil person at his evil deeds; and it must be admitted also that there is something agreeable in the evil person's pain when it results from someone else's pleasure. Just think what you would feel upon discovering that the cheerful friend whose good mood has boosted your mood has just come back from a torture session in which he took particular relish. You would not, I venture to suggest, go on sharing his pleasure. If you are evil yourself, on the other hand, then you will have a more complicated reaction: you won't relish your friend's pleasure since it is pleasure, though you will gain some small *frisson* from the fact that it was at least produced by someone else's pain.

This point shows, incidentally, that it is false that pleasure is always a good thing and pain a bad thing: the pain-produced pleasure of the evil person is not good, and his pleasure-produced pain is not bad. It all depends on what the pleasure and pain are pleasure and pain *at*—what their content is. I do not think that a world in which people systematically enjoy other's pain is better than a world in which sympathetic pain is felt, even though there is more pleasure in the first world. The rule of maximizing pleasure therefore has to be restricted to rule out cases of evil pleasure.

I mean the analysis to be a useful schema for thought, not a fully adequate piece of human psychology. It oversimplifies in a number of ways and ignores subtle distinctions between cases, but I think it lays bare a useful structure for reflection. It idealizes the phenomena in somewhat the way standard decision theory does. That is why I started with the two imaginary species. We can add refinements and qualifications to it as we apply it to concrete cases. It permits us to raise the right questions, as we shall see below.

Death is not cited as one of the evil person's objects. Again, we could add this as a disjunct, but I think it is helpful not to because it introduces a different syndrome of evil. The kind of evil character I am interested in may regard killing as not at all what he desires. His pleasure is specifically in the suffering of others and death puts an end to the possibility of suffering. The paradigm is the torturer: he wishes to keep his victim alive and conscious and may be disappointed and chagrined when the victim accidentally expires. Also, much evil is simply not so extreme as to seek death; and we risk not naming it correctly if we think that evil must always involve a desire to kill. Of course, the suffering of death or dying fits the analysis we already have, but the mere fact of extinguishing a life may not be on the agenda of the evil agent. He finds no pleasure in the thought of everybody dying painlessly in their sleep, even if he is the agent of that event.

3. SOME APPLICATIONS

Which phenomena are captured by the analysis? Pleasure in violence is the obvious case, and probably the most central. The violent sadist is precisely someone whose pleasure results from the pain of the other. The violence need not be physical; there are psychological sadists too. Nor is it confined to the pages of psychiatric journals: sadism of greater or lesser degree is common and not even frowned upon. Violent sports certainly tap into it, as do violent films, and speech designed to wound is just a special case. The sadistic impulse that used to express itself in public executions, inquisitions, bear baiting, and so on now finds subtler outlets, but the essential mark of it is there—pleasure taken in the harm that comes to others.[4] In any case, pleasure in the infliction of pain by means of physical violence is the prime example of evil in the defined sense.

Envy and *schadenfreude* ('malicious enjoyment of others' misfortunes', as the dictionary candidly says) also fit under the analysis, and they illustrate the need for the pleasure-to-pain link. In envy, pangs of distress are occasioned by the success or happiness of others, and *schadenfreude* is just the reverse side of this. It is interesting to ask how much sadistic evil comes from envy and its kin: in order to stem the pain of envy it is necessary to reduce the other to an unenviable state, and this requires harm and unhappiness for the other. Generalized envy of others could easily lead to a personality that seeks the suffering of others (we

---

[4] It might be objected that our interest is really in a set of activities that *de facto* cause harm, not in the harm itself. But it is highly doubtful that we would show the same interest in activities that were similar but did *not* cause harm (as it might be, injury-free boxing). The pain and danger are part of the intrinsic appeal of violent sports, for both players and spectators.

shall come back to this). In any event, envy comes out as evil by my analysis—a vice, as is traditionally taught. It shares its basic structure with sadism. Claggart is described as envious of Billy's moral nature, and Melville remarks upon the shamefulness that is associated with envy—no one will admit to it. This shamefulness might plausibly be linked to the fact that envy fits the pattern that defines evil, and that is not something readily confessed. Nevertheless, envy is a common emotion, so the psychological structure that defines evil is quite widespread. Note that it must be pain at the happiness of others just because of that happiness; feelings of injustice that someone else has what you justly deserve are a different matter (the former often represents itself as the latter).

Revenge and rivalry present interesting cases because of the ambivalence that attends them. In revenge we seek the suffering of the other for his evil deeds: we thus derive pleasure from the other's pain, justly administered. This makes revenge fall into the category of evil, but it is also a case in which justice is done. So it partakes of both good and evil. We tend to resolve this tension by demanding that no real *pleasure* be taken in the demise of the miscreant; a stern and lofty judiciousness is recommended. Yet a furtive smile is apt to break through this resolve as the villain receives his just deserts. We feel uncomfortable about revenge because it partakes rather too strongly of the evil impulse—and of course much evil is done under its banner. Revenge comes too close to what it is meant to punish. One of the subsidiary evils brought about by evil agents is that they force upon others, by way of just revenge, a psychology that virtue would prefer to shun. Violent acts lead to violent reactions in the vengeful. In extreme cases, the desire for just revenge can convert a person's hedonic dispositions from virtuous to vicious in a fairly systematic way: the person becomes obsessed with visiting suffering on the original villains. Hence the ambivalence about revenge and the special moral dangers it carries.

Rivalry brings similar dangers. In the nature of the case the rivals seek to better each other: the failure of the other is part of what is intended, and this is bound to involve pain for the loser. Thus winning, which is pleasurable, necessarily involves pain for the vanquished. In competition, then, we are prone to be caught up in the kinds of psychological links that characterize evil: the pain of others is the occasion of our pleasure, and their pleasure goes with our pain. And the more violent the competition the closer will the participants' psychology approximate to that of the sadist (consider boxing). If this psychology persists outside the arena of competition, then it is likely to spill into other areas. And given that competition exists at so many levels, any culture that encourages it is risking the proliferation of the evil psychology. The notions of winning and losing, when generalized, become forces for creating the wrong hedonic dispositions. Again, ambivalence is the natural attitude. If pleasure and winning become psychologically intertwined, then pleasure will tend to come only at the expense of others' pain. So if we want to encourage pleasure in others' pleasure, then the social pattern of rivalry is the wrong basis. A culture dominated by sports is going to be one in which this danger is routinely courted. At the least, countervailing forces need to be instituted if the wrong psychology is not to be reinforced (hence the traditional insistence on the virtues of 'good sportsmanship').[5]

4. THE EXPLANATION OF EVIL

It is sometimes said that there is something mysterious and inexplicable about the evil character: his motivation makes no sense to us. What is the *point* of evil? We can see the point of instrumental evil, because this is subsumable under egoism. But what possible benefit comes from pure evil—the production of pain for its own sake? What does the evil agent *get* out of that? The virtuous character, by contrast, is not supposed to be enigmatic, because we can explain the appeal of good acts by the simple fact that they are *good*—they have morality on their side. When I perform an altruistic act my motivation is precisely to cause well-being in others, and that seems sufficiently explanatory. There is

---

[5] The need for good sportsmanship thus goes deeper than mere 'gentlemanly behaviour'; it is essential to counteracting the psychological perils inherent in striving for victory over others. Shaking the hand of the loser is a way of saying: 'I am not glad that you are unhappy.' Triumphalism and the decline of civility on the sports field are thus signs of a deeper malaise. We must always insist upon a sharp distinction between proper and improper competitiveness (I include the seminar room here as much as the football field or boxing ring).

an obvious point in creating happiness, no matter whose it is, since happiness is good. But we cannot explain the appeal of evil acts simply by saying they are *bad*—that morality is *against* them. That hardly tells us what positive point there is in their being performed. There appears to be an explanatory asymmetry here, which makes the explanatory question for evil pressing. That an act has good effects can explain why an agent performed it, but the bad effects of an act cannot explain why it was performed— though there exist both types of act. Moral value is explanatorily asymmetrical. No doubt this reflects the fact that goodness, but not badness, can *justify* an action; but then the question remains what can possibly be prompting the evil act, if not the moral justifiability of its object. What sort of motive is this?

I shall explore this question in terms of the analysis given so far. Why is it that some people are subject to the psychological law that pain in others causes pleasure in them? Is there some sort of 'deep structure' to this type of psychology that makes sense of it? Is it perhaps derivative from some other psychological law or syndrome? We can consider several possible answers to this question.

One answer, historically prominent, is that there is a dark Satanic force that underwrites this law. The devil intrudes upon our psychology to make us prefer the pain of others to their pleasure. In extreme cases Satan actually takes possession of us, substituting his psychology for ours. This is a religious answer. I shall not discuss this answer in any depth, mainly because I do not accept the background religious assumptions. Let me just note that the answer does not really explain what needs to be explained anyway. It does not tell us what the evil person finds appealing about the pain of others; it simply offers to tell us what causes him to come to have evil impulses to begin with. Moreover, the invocation of the devil simply raises the same question about *his* psychology: why does he find the pain of others worth pursuing? The devil's psychology raises our puzzle in its most intense form, without resolving it. What *does* make Satan tick? It is no answer to say that he is Satan. So this kind of explanation cannot satisfy us.

A second answer is that some explanation of a naturalistic kind obtains, but it is beyond human powers of comprehension to fathom it. Evil is a natural mystery; its explanation lies too deep in nature for our paltry minds to penetrate. I am not against this kind of position in other areas,[6] but in this area it seems out of place. Surely the explanation must lie closer to what is being explained, since it must supply some kind of *rationale* for the evil impulse—something that makes sense of the agent's surface motive. How could what makes sense of that motive not make sense to its bearer? In any case, this position should be a response of last resort; so we need to see whether we can do better with other approaches.

A third answer is that the explanation lies at the level of neurology and biochemistry: there are brain circuits of a purely physical kind that dispose the agent to feel the way he does about the feelings of others. We therefore need to do some brain science to find out what makes people evil. This answer is not mistaken in its substantive assumptions; no doubt there is some differential neural correlate for the two types of hedonic disposition. We might indeed eventually discover the neurophysiological basis of evil. But again, the explanation is at the wrong level to satisfy us: we want to know what it is *psychologically* that underwrites the evil disposition. Neural correlates cannot make sense of it in the way we would like.

A fourth answer is that the explanation lies at the level of ordinary folk psychology, perhaps augmented with some theoretical extensions. The explanation is thus implicit in our ordinary grasp of human motivation, at least as to its general shape. The hedonic law holds because of further desires the agent has, from which the desire to cause pain results as a means of satisfying those further desires. We need, then, to identify which desires these are. I shall discuss this kind of answer in some detail, after mentioning the final answer I want to consider.

This final answer is that the law is simply brute and basic, having no further explanation at all. On this view, evil is inexplicable simply in the sense that any basic law of a special science is. This position seems to be implicit in Melville's story, since Claggart's evil is 'according to nature' and nothing is said to resolve it into anything more comprehensible. There may indeed be a physical realization of it in Claggart's brain, but there is nothing illuminating that can be said at the level of folk psychology. In a sense,

[6] See McGinn, *Problems in Philosophy*, in which many mysteries are embraced as inevitable.

the evil motive is primitive: that is just the way some people *are* as a matter of brute nomological fact. I shall also be considering this answer in some depth.

5. THE ATTRACTION OF PAIN

Suppose I desire to cause you pain, so that I get pleasure when my desire is satisfied. This is not *for* anything, such as to force valuable information out of you or punish you for a crime. I simply have sadistic impulses towards you—I find your suffering enjoyable. Might this desire for your pain be a means of satisfying some deeper desire I have, so that your pain is instrumental in satisfying that deeper desire? It is not that I simply desire you to *feel* pain, period; rather, your feeling pain will be accompanied by something *else* I desire. There are a number of suggestions that are sometimes made to this effect; let us review them.

It might be supposed that what I deeply desire is to be noticed, remembered, paid attention to, and that causing you pain is how I choose to bring this about. Pain is certainly something that has an impact on people, the spectator as well as the sufferer, so that causing it is sure to get me noticed. Others may well hate me for causing the pain, but they will surely not be indifferent to me. I will have made inroads into their mental life. In extreme cases, I may become nationally famous, a criminal celebrity—I will go down in history. Causing suffering is my way of satisfying this desire for notoriety.

A parallel type of theory is that by causing you pain I assert my power over you, remove your freedom, make of you a mere body. Pain is a means to domination of the other. I desire such domination—such asymmetry of power—and producing pain is the way to achieve this. What I primarily want from you is helplessness, and causing you pain will collapse you into a helplessly writhing body. This is Jean-Paul Sartre's answer to what he aptly calls 'the problem of sadism': the sadist 'seeks to utilize the Other's body as a tool to make the Other realize an incarnated existence'[7]—to make the other's consciousness no more than consciousness *of* the body. For in this condition the other will be

---

[7] Jean-Paul Sartre, *Being and Nothingness*, 399.

reduced to a mere 'in-itself', a being without freedom. On this theory, I cause you pain because of this further desire I have—pain is a good way to achieve that further aim. I seek to destroy your freedom, and I choose pain as my means to this end.

The trouble with these kinds of theory is pretty obvious. The proffered explanations may do something to take the mystery out of the sadist's psychology, and they have the effect of making his desires seem marginally less repellent and disturbing, but they suffer from the problem that causing pain is not the *only* means of achieving the ends in question. If these explanations were correct, then the evil agent could just as well choose benign ways to achieve his deeper aims; but that is surely to underestimate his attachment to the evil he perpetrates. I might get myself noticed and remembered in any number of different ways—for example, by being exceptionally virtuous or skilled at ping-pong or by spectacular hara-kiri. It is surely implausible to suggest that the evil character chooses to cause pain in others just because it is a quicker or more convenient way to be noticed; no, he *likes* causing pain, for its own sake. It isn't that he is indifferent as to whether pain or something else will satisfy his craving for attention; his motive is specifically directed to pain. Pain is not merely a *means* to something logically independent of it.

The same problem applies to the Sartrean theory, since there are other ways of reducing a person to their body aside from producing pain. Pleasure can do that too, especially sexual pleasure. Helplessness can accompany such pleasure. But the sadist is not someone who would just as happily choose producing pleasure in furtherance of his desire to reduce the other to a body; his choice of pain is not just a dispensable means to a logically independent end, but an end in itself. Sartre is aware of this consequence of his theory, but he tries to make a virtue out of it by insisting that in sexual desire, 'I orient myself in the direction of sadism' (404)—a delightfully cagey way to put the problem it poses for him. On Sartre's theory, there ought to be no real distinction between the desire to produce sexual pleasure and the desire to produce pain, since both equally incarnate the other as flesh. But this makes the sadist's attachment to pain quite incidental. It also wrongly locates sadism purely in the sexual sphere, as if it could have no other manifestation. But cruelty can take many forms, not all of which have a sexual dimension, no matter how generous we are with the notion of the sexual. And how is the Sartrean theory to deal with purely mental cruelty, since here there is no mortification of the flesh designed to reduce the victim to his body? What about the intellectual sadist? What of emotional torture?

There is a pattern here: any theory that tries to treat causing pain as a means to satisfying some further desire will face the problem that pain is valued for itself by the evil person. So such theories have a basic structural weakness. Still, there does seem to be a question in this vicinity that cries out for an answer: what is it exactly that makes the pain of others attractive and pleasurable? What are the properties of pain that recommend it to the evil person? No further independent *desire* needs to be satisfied by producing or witnessing pain, but is there some characteristic of pain that makes its appeal intelligible? It is not a mere instrument to some other end, but maybe we can still explain its capacity to enthral.

The Marquis de Sade, that proponent and anatomist of pain, thought its mere intensity was enough to explain its appeal: 'It is simply a matter of jangling all our nerves with the most violent possible shock. Now, since there can be no doubt that pain affects us more strongly than pleasure, when this sensation is produced in others, our very being will vibrate with the resulting shocks.'[8] And again: 'No kind of sensation is keener and more active than that of pain; its impressions are unmistakable.'[9] His idea, then, is that the pain of another has more *energy* in it, and hence acts as a more powerful stimulus on the observer—all that screaming and shouting and writhing! But it is implausible to think that the sadist chooses pain as his source of stimulation simply because it is more *forceful* than pleasure. That is too extrinsic a feature of pain, which leaves the sadist happy to produce pleasure so long as it matches pain in intensity. Given a choice between producing a mild pain and an intense pleasure, he will choose the pleasure, on this account. (Was Sade perhaps a nicer man than he represented himself as being?) We clearly need to find a feature of pain

[8] Quoted by Simone de Beauvoir in her introduction ('Must we Burn Sade?') to Sade's *The 120 Days of Sodom and Other Writings*, 20. For readers innocent of Sade's writings, let me say, by way of warning, that they are for the most part absolutely disgusting.
[9] Ibid., 23.

that other sensations *cannot* have. Nor is its power to suffuse a person's consciousness enough, since this can be achieved by other means—orgasm can do that, or aesthetic rapture. We need a causal power of pain that is unique to it.

Some light can be shed on this by noting that severe pain can have the result that the sufferer ceases to value his life. If the pain is bad enough, he would rather die than endure it. And even if the pain is not that severe, it is still true that one values one's life *less* when it is a life of pain. Now this is a state of mind in which the person has rejected one of his deepest values, perhaps the deepest—his attachment to life itself. He no longer values his life above all else, but is prepared to lose it in exchange for the cessation of pain. So the inflicter of the pain has caused his victim to give up one of his deepest values; he has disrupted in a fundamental way the value-structure of the victim. What was once most precious has become a heavy burden. No kind of pleasure can do this, no matter how intense it may be. Quite the opposite—pleasure only increases one's attachment to life. Here we have the kind of asymmetry between pleasure and pain that we are looking for. So part of the sadist's intention seems to be to effect this kind of rejection of the basic value of life. The torturer most relishes the moment when he causes the victim to renounce even the value of his own life. This is certainly a profound form of power over another, and power does seem to be one of the things sought by the sadist. It is not merely the power of life and death; it is the power to make someone invert the values they assign to these two conditions. The sadist wants the other to *want* death. And even if he is not of this extreme type, he relishes the diminution of value the victim attaches to his life.

If this is right, we can notice an affinity between cruelty and two other things—sexual seduction, and rhetorical persuasion. It is not that any of these is a special case of any of the others; rather, they each instantiate the same abstract pattern. In seduction, especially of the innocent or reluctant, the object is made to abandon his normal values and desires by being swept up in bodily ecstasy. Sexual sensations cause a disruption of the standing order of value assignments. And the pleasure of seduction is commonly held to be enhanced by this, precisely because it involves a fundamental transformation of the object's value structure. (This is very evident in Choderlos de Laclos's *Les Liaisons*

Dangereuses, in which subverting the chaste values of Madame de Tourvel is deemed a great prize.)[10] The value of innocence or abstinence or fidelity is usurped by the seducer as he creates a bodily and mental state that pushes such scruples aside. Seduction of the reluctant differs crucially from brute rape in this respect, since rape will not normally involve any suspension of standing values in the victim. The dictionary meaning of 'to seduce', in its broadest sense, is precisely 'to persuade (person) into abandonment of principles'. So there is a certain abstract analogy between seduction and sadism. It is not that sadism and sexual seduction are somehow equivalent or tap into the same psychic formations, but it is true that they share the characteristic of transforming the other's ordering of values. Both involve making the other want what he normally does not want, and in a fundamental way.

Discursive persuasion, when sufficiently far-reaching, has the same abstract character: the person's basic convictions are radically altered. Consider arguing a person out of their core religious or moral beliefs—persuading a theist there is no God, or an atheist that there is one. Suddenly the person's deepest beliefs are no more, replaced perhaps by those of the persuader. This is a rare and enticing form of power, because it is so transformative of the person being persuaded; and even less extreme kinds of conversion have their proportionate appeal. Perhaps it is no accident that some forms of this are referred to as 'brow-beating', since a certain psychological violence attaches to them, and even perfectly rational and gentle persuasion can be felt as a threat to psychic equilibrium. It is, after all, the replacement of one set of adherences by another, with the psychic upheavals attendant upon this. Rhetorical power is the power to cause psychic revolutions, rearrangements of cognitive and affective structure. This, again, resembles the power of the sadist, as he causes the victim to re-evaluate his attachment to life.

Sadism, seduction, and persuasion thus share a common abstract structure. They each involve power over the values of another person. Sade himself exhibited all three tendencies to an extreme degree—being a proselytiser, a seducer of the unwilling, and (of course) a sadist. We might think of sadism as the most ex-

---

[10] Great pleasure is also taken in informing her of her betrayal, thus linking seduction with sadism.

treme form of the pattern of all three, in which the victim rejects even the value of being alive. Pain is used to cause an abandonment of the deepest of principles. Granted this abstract affinity, some psychological predictions suggest themselves. Is the sadist typically someone lacking in seductive or persuasive power, who makes up for this in the only way he is able? Do we find that the sadist is someone with a shaky or shifting attachment to his own values who wishes to cause the same disequilibrium in others? Does he tend to disvalue his own life because of the pain *it* contains? Is the compulsive persuader also inclined to cruelty? Is the need to seduce the unwilling an expression of cruel impulses? How often do human relationships begin with persuasion, move on to seduction, and end in cruelty?

But the existence of this trilogy should not make us think that the sadist is unattached to pain *per se*, that he would as happily be a seducer or a persuader. What is peculiar to pain is the particular value it tends to undermine, not the fact that it undermines *some* deep value. It causes a rejection of the value of life, and nothing but pain seems capable of this (remember that more than physical pain is in question here: boredom and depression can count as pain in our broad sense). Indeed, pain can cause the sufferer to *hate* his life, to curse (as we say) the day he was born. This is a very radical disruption—a total inversion—of a person's normal value structure. This is what the cruel person achieves, and it is indeed an awesome power. Note that it is an achievement that works only so long as the victim is alive and conscious; so death is not the object at all. There is, then, something in the old idea that sadism and power are connected, but we need to be specific about *what* it is a power to do. It is not merely a power to reduce a person to his body or to control his consciousness; it is a power to bring the person to desire death, in extreme cases, and to lessen his attachment to life, in less extreme cases. The sadist is able to relish his own attachment to life with added piquancy while he causes another to relinquish that attachment. He can compare his own life to that of the victim and be joyful at the disparity in well-being.

Here is where envy makes its unholy alliance with cruelty. The sadist's project can act as a radical antidote to deep existential envy, and even milder forms of cruelty can serve to alleviate the pangs of envy. This helps explain why the beautiful and virtuous are often considered such ripe targets for cruel treatment. Envy of virtue and beauty is certainly part of what motivates Claggart against the 'Handsome Sailor'—he cannot abide the disparity in their natural endowments. Fortunate people will be apt to value life more highly than less fortunate ones, sometimes because of the value that resides *in* them; they will experience more pleasure and less pain. Billy Budd is depicted as remarkably content with his lot, always cheerful and agreeable, despite the fact of his impressment and lowly station. Causing such a person to value his life less, even to the point of hating it, serves to reduce the envy of the less generously endowed. Suppose you find yourself in misery because of someone else's happiness; you will then find life less valuable than the object of your envy finds it. You will feel the need to redress the imbalance; and causing pain is the obvious way to do it. Envy of others' happiness is a source of mental pain, and the way to reduce this pain is to make others less happy. The confirmed sadist may thus be someone suffering from a kind of existential envy—a feeling that his life is intrinsically less valuable than other people's. His life project, then, is to reduce the well-being of others to his dismal level. The sadist has found a brutally simple solution to the problem of envy. The pain of others has the unique power to expunge envy. We find it hard to be envious of even the most fortunate of people if they are in constant intense pain. Painful illness in others is a balm to the envious, pre-empting the need to cause misery oneself, with the risks and moral infamy attendant upon that.

We might expect, then, to find cruelty in the constitutionally envious. To such individuals evil is the only route to happiness, given that they must erase the disparity that so distresses them. Sade may be viewed as someone who saw this clearly and refused to flinch from it: his own happiness lay precisely in the misery of others, because happiness in others was an affront to his own less than felicitous condition. Someone convinced of the inherent misery of mortal life, but seeing that others are unable or unwilling to share his clear-sightedness, may be so moved by envy as to seek the suffering of others. Why should they be blindly happy when I am unable to be? If I see that life is not worthwhile, but you insist against all the evidence that it is, thus preserving some equanimity, I may be moved by envy to make your life *really* miserable—obviously and unmistakably so.

Causing intense bodily pain is then the obvious method to choose. It was lucky for Sade that pain exists, for otherwise he would have had no obvious way to soothe the rages of his envy. A mere twist of the arm can make life unbearable for the duration. Pain is the devil's gift to the envious. It permits retribution for the misery of the envy inflicted by others.

There is therefore some intelligible psychological structure surrounding delight in the pain of another: the other's pain does something for me. It is not that the mere *quale* of pain holds some primitive fascination for me when occurring in someone else. The sadist's project is also one that can be fulfilled; unlike on the Sartrean theory, according to which the sadist cannot fulfil his aim, because freedom can never be annihilated and the person never made wholly flesh while still conscious. Sartre takes the sadist's project to be self-contradictory in the end—which is surely a mark against his analysis of it. On my analysis, sadism makes perfect sense: it has a coherent goal and a method of achieving that goal. To be sure, it is evil—but it is at least intelligibly evil.

The account also has the desirable feature of not sanitizing or softening the sadist's psychology: his governing impulse is about as repulsive as any could be—to make another person not want to live. This is a good deal more heinous than merely wanting to make one's mark on the world or reduce the other to fleshly existence. What the sadist is primarily aiming at is the desire system of the victim—he wants to alter it from being pro-life to being anti-life. He does not primarily seek the death of the victim, only the victim's desire for his *own* death. The victim's suicide is the logical extension of the sadist's aim, but this has the disadvantage that the victim will no longer exist in a state of complete value-turnaround. The death of the victim is always a matter for profound ambivalence on the part of the sadist: it is both consummation and failure.

6. PRIMITIVE EVIL

I have not maintained that envy *must* be what invariably lies behind the sadistic impulse, though it seems to me that this is commonly so. There may be yet 'purer' cases of cruelty in which more detachment from the victim obtains (cruelty to animals may qualify for this category, though here, too, generalized envy may have its place).[11] It certainly does not seem to be a conceptual truth, or a platitude of folk psychology, that cruelty is invariably motivated by envy. If it is, then indeed it makes sense in terms of the agent's pursuit of his own well-being. But isn't there also the purest of all cases, in which the agent seeks the other's pain simply for what it does to the *other*, not for any spin-off for the agent? He feels no envy of the other, so has no egoistic motive to reduce the other's happiness; he just wants the other to suffer, *period*. His pleasure in the pain of the other is psychologically primitive. It is just a brute fact about him (in both senses) that he gets his 'kicks' from the suffering of others. He desires the suffering of others as primitively as he desires his own happiness. The intentional content of his other-directed desires is simply 'to give him pain', just as the intentional content of his self-directed desires is 'to give myself pleasure'. Perhaps the very evil of the malicious desire is what gives it potency: the agent aims at pain *because* it is bad to do so. Badness is seen as a reason for performing the act. The altruistic agent finds the well-being of others attractive to his will, while the evil agent is likewise attracted to the distress of others. Psychologically, both are primitive affective and conative structures. Neither impulse can be seen as an expression of ordinary egoistic motives.

This is in effect to say that the hedonic dispositions of the purely evil person are primitive. It can be a primitive fact about someone that their own pleasure (attachment to life) is reinforced by the pain (*de*tachment from life) of another, just as it can be a primitive fact about someone that their pleasure is reinforced by the pleasure of others. This is, as it were, simply how they *are*. Of course, a person with the evil disposition might well contrive some sort of rationalization of his psychology: he might even erect an ethical system in which his type of disposition is celebrated. Individualism and notions of authenticity can sometimes lead to this kind of ethical position. But this is really *ex post facto*;

---

[11] I suspect that envy of animals is actually quite deep-seated, and may account for the sadistic manner in which they are often treated. It is easy to feel envy at the fact that the life of a wild animal is free, comparatively serene, and unencumbered by ethical restraints—in stark contrast to so many human lives. Animals don't even have to go to work!

the evil disposition comes first. It is psychologically primitive, even if it can be shown to be intellectually derivative. That is, it is not derived from some other sort of desire to which it is related merely as means. The desire to do harm can be a basic desire, just as the desire to do good can be, or the desire to benefit oneself. It is the third-person counterpart of another sort of desire seldom mentioned in inventories of human motives: the desire to harm oneself. This desire too must be found room for, and its existence not defined away. Not all human motivation is aimed at producing the good, in oneself or others, despite the utopianism of some philosophers. Harm can be an end in itself.

Decisions are therefore not the result of a conflict between selfish and altruistic desires alone; malicious desires also enter the decision-making process, as indeed do self-destructive desires. Maximizing *dis*utility can be an aim in itself. The evil character is such as to value life to the degree that others are made to disvalue it. His pleasure is your pain. The question is: is this any more difficult to accept than that the dispositions of the virtuous person are primitive, or those of the thoroughgoing egoist? We tend to think that deriving pleasure from pleasure needs no special explanation—it is 'natural', just what we would expect, intrinsically intelligible. We value pleasure in others because it *is* valuable. But (we tend to think) deriving pleasure from pain is 'unnatural', counterintuitive, intrinsically mysterious. It is a bit like the way we tend to think (erroneously) of homosexuality and heterosexuality: that the latter needs no special explanation, while the former does. Evil is taken to be the anomalous member of the pair.

I think that the assumption of asymmetry here is mistaken, at least if construed conceptually (statistically evil is probably rarer). Neither hedonic law is more intrinsically intelligible than the other, not when you get right down to it; both are basic and brute from the point of view of folk psychology. So there is nothing *more* mysterious about acting on the evil disposition than acting on the virtuous one. (Of course, the latter is more *justifiable*, but that is another question.) In fact, if anything, the boot is on the other foot, since evolutionary considerations tend to predict the evil type of psychology. It is, then, just a fact that some people are hooked up so as to derive pleasure from others' pain, while other people are hooked up differently. Sympathy for the pain of others, rather than relish of it, is not in any way distinctively psychologically transparent: these are just two different ways in which characters may be constituted. Vice is no more enigmatic than virtue. It may be much harder morally to accept the existence of pure evil, but from an explanatory point of view it is on all fours with virtue.

I am not saying that there are no reasons why a psychology is formed in one way rather than the other; there may indeed be environmental or even genetic reasons why an individual acquires a particular moral psychology. Early traumas, bad examples, sexual abuse, endocrine imbalance—any of these might predispose a person to develop the evil disposition. But, similarly, the virtuous disposition will also have its psychological causes—a harmonious home, exemplary role models, optimal serotonin. Both sorts of disposition will have their causes, and the effects are not somehow more natural in the virtuous case than in the vicious case. Moreover, to assign a cause to the evil disposition is not to render it derivative from some other kind of motive. My point is that evil is primitive in that latter sense, not in the sense that it has no cause. And the same holds for virtue.

It is as if the agent has a kind of existential choice as to whether, in being aware of others' pain, he is going to feel pain himself or pleasure. Morality recommends the former, it goes without saying, but there is nothing in the natural facts themselves to incline the agent in one direction rather than the other. It is not that pain has written into it, as a matter of natural necessity, the law that associates it with my sympathetic pain rather than my pleasure. In going the evil way I do not go against the grain of nature into a region of deep mystery, while if I go the virtuous way I am following the natural flow of things and keeping the world nice and simple. Viewed naturalistically, why *shouldn't* your pain produce pleasure in me? It isn't as if each pain has inscribed upon it, 'Not to be used for the production of pleasure.' There is, as it were, a kind of radical contingency about which interpersonal pleasure-pain links get established. Conceptually, you can have one just as well as the other. This is, no doubt, quite shocking, but it seems to me indicated by impartial scrutiny of the case. No conceptual truth can save us from the evil character—alas.

7. THE RATIONALITY OF EVIL

Suppose you had the choice of which type of character to be, good or evil. Which would it be more rational to choose, speaking purely egoistically? (Let this be a forced choice, so that you cannot choose to be simply selfish.) Assume, that is, that you are out to maximize your own pleasure, which type of character would be most likely to achieve that goal? Given that both types derive pleasure from something, the question is which of the two will produce the greater amount of pleasure. Reflection on this question does not deliver very comforting conclusions. If there is much pain in the world in which you are destined to live, or it is easy and relatively risk-free to cause it, then it is rational to choose to be evil, since then you will stand to derive a lot of pleasure from the available pain. But if pleasure preponderates, then virtue is the smarter choice. So you have to weigh up how much suffering life will contain and decide accordingly. How much disease and depression is there, how much grief and grind, how much despair and violence? How bad does the prospect of inevitable death make people feel? A pessimistic assessment will naturally lead to a choice of the evil disposition. If life is a vale of tears, then you may as well get some pleasure out of this fact. If, on the other hand, life is full of joy, then you should choose a disposition that responds to that fact with pleasure. It is not easy to settle the question of how good human life is, but there is surely enough on the negative side to suggest that the choice of the evil disposition might well be the more sensible (which is *not* to say the more moral), especially if there is scope for generating more pain from one's own actions. A relevant question here is how many evil people the world is likely to contain. The more evil people there are around you, the more suffering there is apt to be, so the wiser it is for you to be evil too, so that you can derive pleasure from the suffering that is produced. This confirms the old adage that evil begets evil. On the other hand, the more virtuous people there are, the smarter it is to be virtuous yourself, because then you will enjoy a lot of sympathetic pleasure at the pleasure that exists. Presumably there comes a threshold point at which it becomes prudent to switch from one disposition to the other. If life becomes bad enough for people in general, perhaps because of an increase in evil agents, then you may as well adopt

the disposition that makes the most of this. Of course, this is all very abstract and artificial, but I think it corresponds to something in the facts of moral sociology: namely, the *contagiousness* of good and evil, the way a group will take on one colour rather than the other. It may only take one very determined evil-doer to bring about enough pain to make others opt to respond to this with pleasure too; and a saintly individual may generate enough happiness within a group for there to be not enough pain left to be the occasion of celebration.

Notice that indifference is not a smart choice, because then nothing about the mental states of others will give you pleasure. That will then cut down on your possible sources of enjoyment. Again, this seems to correspond to the empirical data: people tend to be virtuous or vicious; sheer indifference is rare and pathological. The indifferent cannot, by definition, be happy. The only advantage to indifference is that it enables you to avoid the pain that comes from the fact that the world contains pain without yourself being positively evil. If you are good, then you get pain from the pain there is, as well as pleasure from the pleasure; while if you are bad, you get pain from the pleasure, as well as pleasure from the pain. In either case you have to suffer some pain. Indifference will spare you this, but only by also excluding pleasure. Perhaps this will seem a good bargain if the sympathetic pain is too great and too frequent, but the cost is high in hedonistic terms. He who sincerely seeks pleasure cannot afford indifference.

Who suffers more, the good person or the bad person? That has long been a vexed issue, with moral optimists insisting that it is the bad person, while gloomier souls fear that the good person is the worse off. The bad person has her conscience to contend with, it is said, while the good person is vulnerable to betrayal and disillusionment. Using the present analysis, we can least frame the question in such a way that we might be able to answer it. The indicated answer is that it ultimately depends upon how much suffering and happiness there actually is. The good person suffers because of the unhappiness he feels at the pain of the world and the success of evil. The bad person has much to relish in the sufferings of his fellow man; his displeasure at the pleasure of others is apt to be less intense. There is something powerful and solid and undeniable about pain and suffering; happiness tends to be fleeting and flimsy, to be just the absence of unhappiness. Here is where Sade's view that pain has the attraction of intensity seems appropriate: trying to derive pleasure from pleasure is like trying to light up a room with a low watt bulb; pleasure lacks the punch that pain carries. From a position of complete neutrality, the intensity of pain certainly recommends it as a potential source of pleasure. It carries the requisite wattage. Thus the evil person can draw upon a high-intensity stimulus as a source of pleasure. The pleasures of the virtuous are apt to be less keen. We may regret these facts, but they do seem to characterize the two types of psychology.

None of the above is meant, of course, to describe how people actually become good or evil. We do not choose our psychologies in the simple way supposed. I have stipulated an idealized thought-experiment with a view to gaining some perspective on the actual facts of moral life. In the light of these reflections, we may well be thankful that human beings do *not* choose their moral psychology in the way specified. To put it differently: the best reason to be moral is just that it is *moral*.[12]

8. THE ORIGINS AND PREVENTION OF EVIL

It approaches tautology to say that one ought not to be evil. The evil character, as I have analysed it, is such as to lead to acts that one ought not to perform. Feeling pleasure at others' pain disposes the agent to perform intentional acts that cause pain in others. So if we want to understand how evil actions come about, and to discourage their existence, we need to investigate how the underlying character is formed. Don't ask: why did he perform that evil action? Ask instead: how did he develop the kind of character that would lead to such actions? That way we go to the root of the matter.

Is there any sense in which a person *chooses* to have an evil character? Correspondingly, does one choose to have a good character? This is a murky question, in which all the puzzles of free will are involved, but I know of no good reason to deny that

---

[12] This reinforces the point made in Chapter 3 that moral truth is not coercive. Morality has no foundation save itself; its justification is internal to it.

choice can influence character, and the idea of this sort of fundamental choice is certainly part of traditional thinking about
virtue. The considerations of the previous section provide a
framework for explicating choice of character: we saw there how
it might be prudentially rational to choose the evil dispositions,
given their hedonistic potential. More realistically, we can imagine a person in the midst of moral life choosing to allow his dispositions to expand in the evil direction, because of the pleasure
he derives from evil actions. We certainly have the idea of affective habits or tendencies being under the control of the will.
Feeling the burdens of compassion and sympathetic suffering,
the agent might decide in favour of indifference, and this in turn
might lead him to go on to choose the livelier mode of the positively evil character. No doubt this is a little understood area of
human psychology, and not part of the canon of contemporary
social science, but it seems to me to be a familiar phenomenon.
We do well to keep our minds open to its possibility.

Still, choice is surely not the only way in which an evil character comes to be exemplified. According to our analysis, this will
happen when something acts to associate pain with pleasure and
pleasure with pain. Perhaps sometimes this has a genetic basis or
component—it may even be the normal genetic tendency, in the
light of evolutionary theory. But there seem also to be factors that
operate more contingently. Let me give two examples of how the
evil link might be set up. Suppose we subject people to displays
of violence while simultaneously entertaining them: they witness
suffering while experiencing the pleasure of entertainment. Then
simple conditioning will associate a pleasurable sensation with
the occurrence of pain in others. Once the association is established, a new occurrence of pain will evoke the same pleasurable
experience, even though no entertainment is being provided. The
reaction of sympathetic pain will be replaced by feelings of pleasure. This could be done either by using actual violence or we
could just use fictional representations of violence. We will thus
establish a lawlike relation between the spectacle of violence and
feelings of pleasure. The evil disposition will then be in place.

And now we can make the obvious point that this is just what
happens with the kind of violent entertainment that is so prevalent and popular. We embed attractive characters in a dramatic
narrative with an upbeat musical soundtrack and excitingly

staged violent confrontations, all at great expense. The result is witnessed with friends in a comfortable theatre with popcorn and Coca-Cola. The audience experiences considerable pleasure as stupendous damage is apparently done to countless individuals. This is highly effective entertainment depicting extreme harm to people. It will hardly be surprising if an association between pain and pleasure is etched into the spectator's nervous system. And the association will be even stronger if countervailing feelings of sympathetic pain are dampened or eliminated by techniques of presentation. I am not saying that the association will inevitably lead to violent behaviour; my point is just that it will set up certain hedonic channels in the person. These channels will predispose him to experience the world in certain ways: he will find himself reacting to actual violence with confused affect, not knowing whether to laugh or cry. In some cases, violent entertainment will interact with a predisposition in the direction of evil to reinforce the connection between suffering and pleasure. According to the present analysis of evil, then, we should be concerned about the psychological effects of violent entertainment. There are real risks in conjoining killing and fun.[13] (Note that there is no comparable concern about sexual entertainment, since this associates pleasure with pleasure—so long, that is, as we are not considering sadistic sexual entertainment.)

The other example is that of group behaviour. For social animals like ourselves, there is pleasure in co-operation, in co-ordinating our actions with those of others. But this pleasure can exist even when what is done is evil—there is still the pleasure of co-operation and fellow-feeling. So doing evil things in groups is bound to set up an association between pleasure on the part of members of the group and the suffering of the victim. This pleasure might be felt by an individual who would not feel it if acting alone. And of course it is commonly observed that people will do much worse things in groups than singly. No doubt conformity is part of this, but it also stems from the fact that group endeavour is inherently agreeable. Any form of communal violence has the

---

[13] The fact that violent films are known by the audience to be make-believe does not alter the hedonic associations they set up—pleasure is still taken in the spectacle of violence. Purer examples of combining entertainment and violence are bull-fighting and boxing—not to mention public torture, cock-fighting, bear-baiting, and all the rest.

powerful force of group enjoyment to sustain it. Being a regular member of such a group will continually reinforce the hedonic links that characterize the evil character. An individual's natural feelings of revulsion for a violent act might well be blotted out by the rush of fellow-feeling that comes from co-operation. This appears to be precisely what happens in the kinds of group violence described in Bill Buford's *Among the Thugs*,[14] in which the joys of group solidarity, centring on a chosen football team, lead to acts of appalling violence against those outside the group. Even planning and executing a murder with others might involve this kind of recruitment of positive affect. The character of a group is thus more prone to the evil configuration than that of an individual. Not for nothing do we fear the gang and the mob.

The practical upshot of this brief and selective discussion is that evil will be discouraged if we break down the hedonic links that constitute it. We might, at the simplest level, reward children for showing pleasure at the pleasure of others and punish them for the opposite reaction. We might strongly penalize group activity whose object is the harm of others, or at least make people aware of the dangers inherent in group enjoyment. We might look critically at the way violence is being converted into entertainment with ever greater proficiency. We should be alert to the possibility that the victim of an evil act, especially a child, might mimic the hedonic links that characterize the abuser: if the victim sees someone deriving pleasure from her pain, she might copy this tendency, mimicry being a mode of learning. In sum, given the analysis of evil I have suggested, we have a format for thinking about these practical questions and some idea about what would incline people in the right direction. We need to work to bring about the right laws of interpersonal affect in people; for in such emotional states lie the fundamental sources of human action.[15]

---

[14] This shocking book also illustrates how other sources of celebration can become recruited into group violence—regional pride, patriotism, the pleasures of shared food and drink. All these combine to produce intense pleasure in the co-ordinated activity that causes massive harm to others. It is highly probable that men have only been induced to fight in armies because of the pleasures of group action; lone battles require a quite different motivational structure, and one much harder to summon.

[15] My emphasis here on sensation and emotion is meant to go against the model of human behaviour suggested by economic decision theory. It is what a

The notions of pain and pleasure have not been favoured by modern psychology and social science, possibly out of misplaced behaviourism. Implicit in everything I have said in this chapter is the conviction that these two hedonic poles are the mainsprings of human behaviour. This was taken to be a truism by classical thinkers, shaping the way questions of moral conduct were formulated, but now it may seem to some antiquated and prescientific. Obviously I disagree. The fact is that we are powerfully attracted to what gives us pleasure and repelled by what causes us pain. One of the main points of this chapter has been to insist on the close connection between evil and pleasure. The evil character is moved by something more than the mere absence of virtue. If we want to understand and eradicate evil, we need to start by acknowledging how good it feels.

person *feels* that predominantly controls his behaviour; desire matters because of what it feels like to have desire satisfied. A conscious agent is first and foremost a centre of pleasure and pain, a bearer of affect. Pure evil will be unintelligible unless its role in the generation of pleasure is acknowledged.

5

Beauty of Soul

1. AESTHETIC MORALITY

I shall begin, prosaically, with some linguistic observations. Two broad categories of moral terms are commonly distinguished: on the one hand, there are very general and abstract terms of moral appraisal that describe little or nothing about the object in question (so-called 'thin' moral terms)—words like 'good', 'right', 'ought'; and, on the other hand, we have terms that are specific and descriptive while also carrying evaluative force (so-called 'thick' moral terms)—words like 'brave', 'generous', 'miserly'. We are urged to take both sorts of moral concept seriously, and to recognize that the second category is in some ways more basic and central to moral discourse.[1] Well and good: our moral vocabulary clearly does have these two compartments, though the line between them may be blurred. But I would like to draw attention to a third category, not assimilable to these two: terms of moral appraisal that have a strongly *aesthetic* flavour. These are almost wholly neglected in standard discussions of moral concepts, for reasons that go deeper than mere arbitrary selectivity—since they suggest a conception of moral thought that is alien to the entire outlook of twentieth-century philosophical ethics. There are many terms of this type: for example, on the positive side, 'fine', 'pure', 'stainless', 'sweet', 'wonderful'; and on the negative side (which is richer), 'rotten', 'vile', 'foul', 'ugly', 'sick', 'repulsive', 'tarnished'.

These words, or their uses in moral contexts, have certain distinguishing characteristics. They are highly evaluative or 'judgemental', expressing our moral attitudes with particular force and poignancy, somewhat more so than words like 'generous' and

---

[1] See Williams, *Ethics and the Limits of Philosophy*, 143–5.

'brave'. Correspondingly, they are less 'descriptive' than those words, telling us less about the specific features of the agent, though they are more descriptive than words like 'good' and 'right'. They convey a moral assessment by ascribing an aesthetic property to the subject. What they give us are *qualities* of character, morally laden, rather than traits of character—almost *styles* of character. They tell us what to expect of a person, morally speaking, without detailing what traits are dominant in him or her— what their particular virtues and vices may be. So these terms fulfil a particular evaluative need, not already covered by the 'thick' and 'thin' moral terms; they are not conceptually redundant or mere stylistic variants. And they populate moral discourse to a surprisingly high degree, as an attentive ear will confirm. We need to ask what perspective on moral evaluation they presuppose. What do they tell us about the nature of the virtuous or vicious agent?

In this chapter I shall expound and defend the following thesis: that virtue coincides with beauty of soul and vice with ugliness of soul. Call this the aesthetic theory of virtue (ATV for short). The prevalence of the terms cited shows that we often express our moral evaluations by using aesthetic predicates of character; the ATV then interprets this as reflecting our implicit commitment to the view that goodness and badness of character are allied to aesthetic qualities of the person. That is what our ordinary ways of speaking suggest, and the ATV holds that this is indeed a correct way to think about virtue and vice. I hope in what follows to remove the impression that this thesis is merely poetic or sentimental, and clearly false if taken as the sober truth. It really is literally true, I shall argue, that moral distinctions coincide with aesthetic distinctions of a special sort.

The idea of an aesthetically based morality is by no means new. In Robert E. Norton's recent book, *The Beautiful Soul: Aesthetic Morality in the Eighteenth Century*,[2] the author meticulously traces the origins and transformations of the idea of moral

---

[2] Norton restricts himself almost entirely to historical questions, venturing little in the way of independent explication. In the end, indeed, he rejects the conception of the beautiful soul for reasons he finds in Hegel (and which I find obscure). The present chapter can be seen as an argument to the effect that such rejection is misplaced. Nevertheless, Norton's book is a valuable study of the tradition I am trying to continue.

beauty from Plato and Plotinus, through to Shaftesbury and
Hutcheson, and on to to Kant, Schiller, Goethe, and Hegel. As he
demonstrates, this conception of the moral life has a rich and var-
ied history, dominating ethical thought for considerable periods,
despite its contemporary academic occlusion. It is an idea that
has attracted the attention, indeed the devotion, of theorists and
ordinary people of many periods and places. Yet it has never received any serious analytical formulation, remaining more of a
nebulous ideal than a precise doctrine. We need to ask what it
means to ascribe beauty to the soul, and to spell out the way this
correlates with moral attributes. In particular, we need to assure
ourselves that the doctrine is conceptually coherent, and thus capable of explaining certain features of morality. It is in this spirit
of constructive critical analysis that I shall be discussing the
topic.

2. REID ON THE AESTHETICS OF THE SOUL

Thomas Reid maintained a pair of challenging theses about
ethics and aesthetics.[3] He held (i) that all aesthetic properties are
derivative from aesthetic properties of the mind or soul or character, and (ii) that moral properties of the person are aesthetic
properties or are conceptually linked to them. As to thesis (i), he
says: 'we ascribe to a work that grandeur which properly is inherent in the mind of the author' (773), so that 'when we consider
the *Iliad* as the work of the poet, its sublimity was really in the
mind of Homer' (773). Hence 'those who look for grandeur in
mere matter, seek the living among the dead' (778). In the same
way, 'The beauty of good breeding . . . is not originally in the external behaviour in which it consists, but is derived from the
qualities of mind which it expresses' (788). According to Reid,
then, the aesthetic quality of an external object consists in its *expressing* an aesthetic quality of mind.

This thesis is the analogue of two other theses: first, that all intentionality or meaning is derivative from mental intentionality,
so that marks on paper and acoustic patterns have their meaning

---

[3] Reid, *Essays on the Intellectual Powers of Man*, Essay VIII. Subsequent page references are to this work.

as a result of that of mental states; and second, that all moral properties are ultimately derived from moral properties of mental states, say of motives or hedonic states, so that actions and states of affairs have their moral properties as a result of the mental states they involve. The three theses together assert the strong primacy of the mental in the aesthetic, semantic, and moral spheres. Physical and perceptible things have these features in a borrowed and dependent way. I shall not further discuss these primacy theses here; I mention them in order to place Reid's position on aesthetics in a recognizable philosophical context. I am in fact sympathetic to all three theses and regard opposition to them as often stemming from an anti-mentalism that is as outdated as it is implausible. In any case, we are going to need a robust conception of mental reality if we are to treat the ATV with any favour.

Reid's second thesis is the thesis I am defending, though it is less well developed in his discussion than the first thesis. He says:

We may therefore justly ascribe beauty to those qualities which are the natural objects of love and kind affection. Of this kind chiefly are some of the moral virtues, which in a peculiar manner constitute a lovely character. Innocence, gentleness, condescension, humanity, natural affection, public spirit . . . these qualities are amiable from their very nature, and on account of their intrinsic worth . . . As they are virtues, they draw the approbation of our moral faculty; as they are becoming or amiable, they affect our sense of beauty. (792)

Thus, 'it is only the expression of the tender and kind passions that gives beauty; that all the cruel and unkind ones add to deformity; and, on this account, good nature may very justly be said to be the best feature, even in the finest face' (803). In these remarks, Reid links together virtue, love, and aesthetic merit, in order to suggest that a virtuous character excites our sense of the beautiful, thus inviting our love.

The view is also suggested by Plato, in the equation of the good and the beautiful—though again it is not developed at all clearly and systematically. Plato does speak of 'beautiful dispositions in the soul',[4] and he famously connects goodness and beauty; so he may be regarded as the father of the ATV. The

[4] Plato, *Republic*, III. 402d.

Oxford English Dictionary also acknowledges the link between beauty and morality by defining 'beauty' as 'combined qualities delighting the senses, the moral sense, or the intellect'. In *Othello* Iago shows his assent to the thesis when he remarks of Cassio: 'He hath a daily beauty in his life that makes me ugly.'[5] He is clearly not referring merely to Cassio's handsome frame here, but sourly expressing his superior virtue.

The conjunction of Reid's two theses has the consequence that beauty of soul is basic aesthetically *and* morally—everything flows from this foundation. He sums up: 'I apprehend, therefore, that it is in the moral and intellectual perfections of mind, and in its active powers, that beauty originally dwells; and that from this as the fountain, all the beauty which we perceive in the visible world is derived' (792). 'Thus the beauties of mind, though invisible in themselves, are perceived in the objects of sense, on which their image is impressed' (794). The beauty that we find in the arts and nature is thus essentially linked to moral ideas, since it reflects beauty of soul, in which virtue in turn consists. The aesthetics of the soul accordingly becomes a central topic of both ethics and general aesthetics, if we follow Reid's view. So if we are attracted by his overall vision, we need to put some work into articulating what such an aesthetics might look like.

Oscar Wilde, the unregenerate aesthete and persistent moralist, alludes to a theory like Reid's in *The Picture of Dorian Gray* (to be discussed in the next chapter). Dorian says to Lord Henry: 'I want to be good. I can't bear the idea of my soul being hideous.' Henry replies: 'A very charming artistic basis for ethics, Dorian! I congratulate you on it. But how are you going to begin?'[6] And the whole story turns on the portrait of Dorian, which depicts his soul, becoming ugly as Dorian sinks into depravity. His soul does become hideous, as the picture reports, even as his good looks never desert him. This story dramatizes the central claim of the ATV: the hideousness of the soul Dorian creates for himself is reflected in an artistic object that is itself hideous; the picture is a concrete expression of inner ugliness, this being equated with evil of character. Wilde is clearly a Reidian about morality.

---

[5] I am aware that I quoted the same line in the previous chapter, but that was to make a quite different point—about envy, not beauty. And it is a good line.

[6] Wilde, *The Picture of Dorian Gray*, 126.

3. ARTICULATING INNER BEAUTY

Let us formulate the thesis a bit more explicitly. The idea is that for a person to be virtuous (or vicious) is for a part or aspect of him—his soul or character or personality—to have certain aesthetic properties: these are necessary and sufficient conditions for personal goodness. Perhaps the best way to conceive of this is by means of a supervenience thesis. Let the supervenience base consist of the various virtues or vices: kindness, justice, generosity, compassion, steadfastness, and so on; cruelty, injustice, meanness, callousness, capriciousness, and so on. And let the supervenient properties be the kinds of morally aesthetic properties we have been considering; for simplicity we might just think of them as inner beauty and ugliness and grades of these. Then the ATV says that the latter properties are supervenient on the former: if two persons are exactly alike with respect to the moral virtues and vices, then they are exactly alike in their morally aesthetic properties; and no one can change their morally aesthetic properties without changing their virtuous and vicious properties. We do not *identify* the aesthetic with the virtuous properties, but we do tie them conceptually together. A natural analogue here is the way the aesthetic properties of a painting supervene on the underlying colour and shape of the paint on the canvas. In both cases we have a combination of base qualities that serve to determine the beauty or otherwise of the object—this beauty being apparent either to the eye or to the moral faculty. So the moral goodness of a person corresponds to these supervenient aesthetic properties. And that is not surprising in view of what they are supervenient upon. The intuitive picture is that the virtues and vices *give rise* to aesthetic properties of the soul that bears them.

It is not, of course, that *all* attributions of aesthetic properties are morally evaluative; the claim is not that music is said to be virtuous when it is described as beautiful. But when the *object* of ascription is a soul (as I shall call the part in question), the aesthetic predicates *become* ethical in purport. Virtue equals beauty *plus* the soul, to put it crudely. The particular *kind* of beauty proper to the soul is what virtue consists in. The notion of beauty needed here must be taken broadly as a catch-all term for a wide range of positively evaluative aesthetic concepts: we mean to include what Reid calls grandeur or magnificence, as well as the lowly aesthetic properties appropriate to smells and tastes.[7] So the thesis is that virtue consists in having positive aesthetic attributes of soul of certain sorts. This nearly, but not quite, precludes the possibility of someone being both evil and having a beautiful soul. As a matter of logic, as opposed to likelihood, it is consistent to suppose that someone has the aesthetic properties constitutive of badness—he has a wide array of foul vices—but also has *other* non-moral aesthetic properties that are sufficient to confer beauty on his soul. We can only rule this out if we specify that *every* aesthetic property of a soul has moral significance. Strictly speaking, we do not need to insist on this, plausible though it is; we need only say that *some* aesthetic properties of soul confer moral status. But I shall stick with the simpler formulation, so assuming that any aesthetic property of a soul has a moral dimension. Also, of course, a person may have some of the aesthetic properties that suffice for goodness (or badness) and not others, so that he is somewhat or partially virtuous (or vicious). For the most part, again, I shall simplify all this by speaking simply of having a beautiful or ugly soul, so that degrees of it won't matter. In any case, the thesis clearly rules out the possibility that a person could be good and have *no* beauty of soul or be bad and be *completely* beautiful of soul.[8]

To evaluate this theory it helps to look at our ordinary lan-

---

[7] Not *all* concepts used in the evaluation of aesthetic works should be included, however. The concept of *originality* would not be appropriate, since it is clearly possible to be vicious in an original way. We need to restrict the relevant concepts to those directly connected to beauty and ugliness. We must also be careful how we interpret notions like grandeur and magnificence: these must not be taken to be equivalent to mere impressiveness or largeness of scale, since some forms of evil can fulfil those descriptions. I take it that in practice it is not difficult to tell when we have cases of genuine beauty; attractiveness and delight are the usual marks of its presence.

[8] The devil is sometimes depicted as having *some* positive aesthetic attributes. He is not always ugly and repulsive, but can be seductive and charming; he may occasionally have refined artistic tastes. But he is never, I think, depicted as genuinely beautiful of soul; his *core* is always repugnant. Such mixed depictions toy with our conceptual associations, trading upon the way we naturally identify the good with the beautiful; they are ironic and playful—conceptual tropes. Nor is the devil figure always depicted as wholly without any of the virtues—he may be brave and loyal and independent of mind. But then he is not completely evil, and may therefore have the aesthetic qualities that go with his virtues. What I would say is that if we *define* the devil as a being lacking all moral qualities, as endowed with every vice, then we shall not be inclined to find *any* beauty in his psychological make-up.

guage of moral appraisal and note how thoroughly saturated it is with aesthetic notions, as I observed at the outset. We may say of a person we morally esteem that she is fine, pure, stainless, of high quality, unblemished, flawless, lovely, delightful, inspiring, simple, natural, spontaneous, sweet, wonderful; while the person we morally disapprobate may be described as rotten, bestial, swinish, stinking, foul, vile, crooked, monstrous, grotesque, sick, sickening, flawed, corrupt, ugly, filthy, shitty, tarnished, disgusting, disgraceful, unclean, repulsive, an asshole, a prick, a cunt.[9] In fact, our vocabulary for describing character in morally evaluative ways is rather impoverished if we do not include these sorts of terms; and it is remarkable, once one attends to it, how common it is to hear moral appraisals expressed in these kinds of aesthetic terms. This richness of morally aesthetic vocabulary certainly invites us to explore the ATV with some seriousness. It can hardly be that whenever we say such things we are uttering outright falsehoods or making silly category mistakes.

Consider, as further data for reflection, the role of physical beauty and ugliness in stories of virtue and vice. In addition to Dorian Gray and his hideous portrait, we have Frankenstein's repulsive creation, Victor Hugo's hunchback of Notre Dame, David Lynch's elephant man, and many others. In each of these cases a contrast is set up between the outward aesthetic appearance and the inner moral quality of the individual. We are invited to look beyond physical ugliness and see that there is still something of beauty within the person. External ugliness is used to set off moral beauty, so that it can be apprehended without the mask of physical beauty. It is the idea of the beautiful soul trapped inside the hideous frame. This conception presupposes two independent aesthetic dimensions to a human being, and by pulling them apart the autonomy of inner beauty is stressed. Then again, whenever there appears a physical embodiment of a person's corrupt and malicious soul it is typically an ugly face that is used to express it. The devil is traditionally conceived as surpassingly hideous. I remember as a child being gripped by the idea of how

[9] There is also a whole category of animal terms, chosen for the supposed repulsiveness of the animal in question: 'vermin', 'rat', 'pig', 'snake', 'insect', 'worm', etc. Then there are the evil and repellent half-animal, half-human hybrids: vampires, werewolves, fly-men, etc. Everything we find aesthetically unappealing seems to find its way into our moral vocabulary somehow.

ugly the devil's face must be and how bloodcurdling it would be
to behold it: evil condensed and folded in on itself, hardly a face
at all. In myths and fairy tales evil almost always comes in a
ghastly form. This is not because of a prejudice against naturally
ugly people; it is the more conceptual thought that the evil person is ugly within—that his *real* face is hideous. We speak of 'the
face of evil', and we try to give this idea visual content. The identification of evil with ugliness of soul is undoubtedly part of common conceptions, as is the identification of virtue with inner
beauty. Embodying evil in a person's physical appearance is simply a vivid way to convey the gruesomeness of their soul.

   We can begin to articulate the conceptual connections
recorded in these cultural and linguistic phenomena by asking
whether it is possible for a soul to be both ugly and virtuous or
beautiful and vicious. Someone might argue that this is logically
possible, holding that these are contingently related properties.
Could not a work of art be aesthetically distinguished yet
morally deplorable? But if that were possible, we ought to be able
to find aesthetic terms that ascribe beauty of soul yet have no
moral implications—morally neutral terms of aesthetic appraisal.
However, ordinary language declines to offer up such terms—
they all seem to have moral import. It is sometimes said that an
evil person can be 'charming', but that is not taken to mean that
his *soul* is charming, just that his manner is; this is really of the
same order as an evil person being physically attractive—which
is certainly possible.[10] A person's *body* can be said to have positive
aesthetic attributes and no moral implications be carried, but I do
not believe we shall find any terms that describe the soul aesthetically that are morally neutral. This seems to me a powerful presumption in favour of the ATV.

   Let us ask what would have to be the case if the ATV were
false. That would mean that a person could present an observer
with both aesthetically positive and morally negative characteris-

---

[10] We can push beauty only so far into a person and preserve his evil. The surface beauty of a bad person is always conceived as a *mask* of some sort—a con-
cealer of inner ugliness. Sometimes we even allow that a given individual can
possess multiple personalities, with some good and some bad, perhaps arranged
in a hierarchy of centrality. In such a case, we have differently characterized aesthetic objects within a single human body. What we do *not* allow is that one and
the same soul can be both thoroughly beautiful and yet morally despicable.

tics, these being instantiated by the same thing, namely, a soul. This would imply that we should be both attracted and repelled by that single thing: we admire the beauty of it but deplore its immorality, valuing and disvaluing it simultaneously. It is not clear how we could realistically do that, since we would be adopting contrary attitudes towards the same object. This would produce dissonance of an extreme kind and it is hard to see how we could preserve both attitudes. As Plato says, we love beauty and hate evil; so we would have both to love and hate the same thing. It is not that this is logically impossible, even in full knowledge of the identity; but it is psychologically highly unnatural. It is hard even to imagine how we could combine these two attitudes towards a single soul. In the case of a person with outward beauty and inner ugliness, we can more easily combine the attitudes of love and hate, because they take distinct objects—the body and the soul—but the idea of a soul that is both loved for its beauty and hated for its vice is far harder to tolerate. This suggests that a convergence of the two sets of characteristics is built into our normal psychology of moral reaction: we would be lost and confused if the two came apart; we proceed on the assumption of their coincidence.

Note further that an evil person will perform ugly actions, most obviously acts of violence, physical or verbal. Violence is inherently ugly and it is the natural manifestation of an evil character. Evil is *expressed* in ugly acts. But it is hard to see how a beautiful yet wicked soul could produce ugly actions, since that would imply that beauty of soul lies behind ugliness in action. The face of the enraged and violent man is not a pretty sight, and how could this stem from inner beauty? Ugly actions reflect ugliness within, but wicked actions are characteristically ugly; so we cannot have the combination of inner beauty and moral badness. The supposed inner beauty would have to be quite cut off from any overt beauty, but this violates the way we think of the relation between character and action. So, again, the supposition of inner beauty combined with evil is reduced to something close to absurdity.

It is also very natural to invoke aesthetic terms in characterizing the possession of the virtues in combination. It is not enough to list the several virtues the good person must possess; we must also say something about how they jointly operate within him or her. Here the traditional term is 'harmony': the virtues must exist severally in the person but must also be harmonious with each other, in a state of balance or equilibrium. Kindness must not override justice, as justice must not erase mercy. Each virtue must occupy its proper place, forming a harmonious whole. There must be an appropriate *order* among the virtues. In one version of this requirement, there must be harmony between the demands of reason or obligation and the promptings of feeling or desire.[11] There must be no collision or dissonance between what we know we ought to do and what we feel like doing. Nothing jagged or jarring must trouble the virtuous soul. But these are aesthetically tinged notions; the notion of harmony has some claim to be *the* central aesthetic notion. No doubt it is a mistake to try to define beauty, but we could do a lot worse than thinking of beauty as consisting in a harmonious whole composed of discrete elements. We might accordingly conceive of the virtuous person as composed of a number of ethical chords, as it were, that blend harmoniously together into a pleasing whole. Thus it is hard to see how someone could be virtuous *tout court* and yet harbour an ugly soul, for the harmony necessary for overall virtue would lift the person out of a state of inner ugliness. Again, we cannot conceptually disconnect the moral and aesthetic dimensions. The picture suggested by our everyday moral vocabulary is thus borne out by these more abstract considerations.

But, it may be objected, all this is just consoling mythology, enshrined in ordinary language. It is a category mistake to think that the soul could be beautiful or ugly; all beauty belongs to the perceptible world, and such beauty has no internal relation to virtue. We are just trying, futilely, to find something to motivate us to be virtuous, now that God is dead and morality itself is admitted to be motivationally weak or inert. We want to connect virtue with beauty so that we can find in virtue something independently attractive and desirable. Instead of the picture of the virtuous person as dry and dull and unappealing, we will have the prospect of finding her to be the very paradigm of all beauty. We all want to be beautiful, vain and sad as we are, and the ATV trades on this all-too-human weakness. Aestheticizing virtue is

---

[11] See Norton, *The Beautiful Soul*, esp. 279–80.

mere wishful thinking built upon an erroneous metaphysics of beauty: so it may be objected.

We can make two replies to this dismissive response, aside from reciting what has been accumulated so far in defence of the ATV. First, recall Reid's expressivism: on his view, no physical thing is intrinsically beautiful; it is so because it expresses in some way a mental act in which beauty primarily resides. This is the doctrine of 'derived aestheticity', analogous to 'derived intentionality'. Now I do not want to try to defend this doctrine here, but it should at least be borne in mind when it is claimed that all beauty resides *outside* the mind. And there is surely something right in Reid's conviction that mere marks on canvas or sequences of sounds could not be beautiful considered purely in themselves.

But we need not follow Reid all the way in order to recognize that aesthetic predicates *can* properly apply to mental realities. It is really only empiricist or anti-mentalist prejudice to suppose otherwise—the presumption that all concepts must be explicable in terms of sensory appearances. After all—and this the second reply—we apply aesthetic predicates to such items as mathematical entities, moves in chess, scientific theories, poetic thoughts, battle plans, philosophical conjectures. Entities of virtually any ontological type can delight our aesthetic faculties. As Reid says, 'Beauty is found in things, so various, and so very different in nature, that it is difficult to say wherein it consists, or what there can be common to all the objects in which it is found' (779). It is not just painting and music and people's bodies and natural landscapes that can be beautiful; virtually anything can be, in its own distinctive way. And it seems to me part of plain common sense to attribute beauty to persons in virtue of their psychological characteristics: when we take delight in a person's presence it is not always their body we are responding to. It can be literally *true* that a person has a beautiful soul, in virtue of the components and operations of that soul—the emotions felt, the thoughts had, the desires experienced. Similarly, it really is hideous to desire the suffering of the innocent, vile to exploit the weak, foul to betray a friend—each of these acts evokes revulsion and disgust in us. We do not respond with mere moral criticism or condemnation; our aesthetic faculties are recruited too. Such aesthetic judgements are as literally correct as comparable judgements about ordinary physical things. And they obviously have moral content.

I am not suggesting that none of this talk is metaphorical. Certainly many of the aesthetic terms we apply to people are metaphors: when we express our moral disapproval of someone by saying that he stinks, for example, we are not supposing that he literally gives off a bad odour. But the same can be said of a work of art: it does not literally stink either, though it may still be *true* that it stinks, aesthetically speaking. Many aesthetic terms are derived from the senses of smell and taste, and are then transferred to objects that are not literally tasted or smelled. The soul is no different in this respect from other aesthetically evaluable objects. My point is that these terms are used univocally in application to these different kinds of object, to express aesthetic evaluations. A soul can be ugly in the same *sense* that a picture or a face is (though not of course in the same *way*). What is literal is the aesthetic component of these often metaphorical terms.[12]

4. ON *BRIEF ENCOUNTER*

We are in imminent danger of taking an idea rooted in common experience and doing it to death with abstract philosophy. So let us pause for a moment to examine the idea in a setting in which it breathes most naturally: the visual medium of film. How better to convey the beautiful soul than through vision and voice and drama? As an illustration, then, of the artistic use of the idea of inner beauty, I shall consider the film *Brief Encounter*.[13] I do not say that the film was intended by its makers to illustrate the concept of the beautiful soul; but I do think this concept suffuses the film and gives it the special poignancy it has.

The story concerns two characters, Alec Harvey and Laura Jesson, who meet by chance in a railway station waiting-room when Alec, a doctor, removes a piece of grit from Laura's eye.

---

[12] If the aesthetic component were merely metaphorical, then we would react to such attributions with mere as-if delight or repulsion. But that is not how we react: our affective responses are entirely serious and 'literal'.

[13] Directed by David Lean, written by Noel Coward, 1946. A discussion of the film (which does not mirror my own) can be found in Richard Dyer, *Brief Encounter*. Naturally, there is no substitute for seeing the film itself.

After a number of meetings they fall in love, despite being both 'happily married'. In the end they decide they must part for the sake of their respective families, and they take leave of each other, irrevocably, in the waiting room in which they first met. The relationship is never consummated, but is extremely intense, and its conclusion is nothing short of tragic. The action is set in provincial England *circa* 1940 in highly unromantic surroundings and is filmed in grim black and white. Dark station platforms, full of noise and smoke, figure prominently. The other characters are notably grey and unappealing, save in a comic way. It is an artless world in which the two lovers meet. But the background music, Rachmaninov's Piano Concerto No. 2, forms a soaring and sublime counterpoint to what is visually presented. We are thus made witness to a realm of beauty existing alongside seediness and mediocrity, hidden but omnipresent. The music exists in the same parallel world in which Alec and Laura exist, so stressing the aesthetic abyss that separates them from their surroundings. They are, or they become, islands of beauty in a drab and dirty landscape.

Laura, played by Celia Johnson, particularly conveys a palpable sense of inner beauty and virtue—so much so that her inner self becomes the central element in the story. This is achieved mainly by focusing on her face, often distinguished by light from dark shadowy surroundings, and by having her speak to us directly in voice-over from her inner being as she recollects the events that have overtaken her. This conjunction of lit face and disembodied voice strongly suggests her spiritual interior and expresses the beauty that lies there. The actress has outer beauty too, though not oppressively so, but the sense of inward quality and grace she projects is what most touches the viewer and makes us understand Alec's passion for her. Humorous, kind, modest, dutiful, sensitive, passionate, extreme—she has beauty of soul of the most transparent kind. (Her husband, Fred, worthily dull, aesthetically challenged, appreciates her in his limited way, but he is blind to the aesthetic phenomenon that sits across the room from him night after night.)

Her natural virtue is what comes into question as she finds herself deceiving her husband and running the risk of ruining the lives of her two children. At one point she is caused to slip out of the back door of the flat where she has come to meet Alec by the

unexpected arrival of his odious and sneering friend. This devious act threatens to tarnish her rectitude and honesty, forcing her
to recognize the kind of life she is in danger of choosing. Her
pure soul is about to become flecked with petty vice. But there is
never really any doubt that her inner beauty remains intact. It is
as if the film is saying: 'Here is the beautiful soul caught in the
quotidian snares of mortal life.' The audience is made to feel that
it can look directly into her soul, see the beauty that is there, and
fear for the deformities that threaten to overtake it. Nothing does
compromise that beauty, despite the sordidness of what surrounds Laura and her own questionable moral position. Alec is
privy to her inner beauty, though not in the immediate way that
the audience is, and he responds to it quickly and strongly. As he
removes the grit from her eye (an apt metaphor for her moral
situation), it is as if he catches a glimpse of her soul and feels its
attractive force. He knows beauty when he sees it; his own good
taste, discreetly conveyed in the film, is what makes Laura attractive to him. The story works so well because her virtue is so perfectly expressed by the inner beauty she displays, to him and us.

Essential to the film's technique is a dualism of aesthetic levels. There is the world of art and feeling, on the one hand, and the
world of dull corporeality, on the other. As the story unfolds, that
outer world becomes less and less real, more dreamlike, as
Laura's inner being comes to occupy the solid centre of the story.
Her inner nature comes to take up more of the world we are witnessing, the seedy surroundings dissolving into a shadowy cartoon-like background. It is as if the beautiful soul is asserting
itself over the world of sense, pressing its claim to reality. The
film is almost a text for the theory we are examining, in the way it
identifies virtue with inner beauty and insists upon a hidden
level of aesthetic reality. The visual medium is uniquely well
adapted to dealing with this theme, because of its ability to translate spiritual beauty into an affair of the eye; the story could not
have worked so well had it been cast in a purely verbal form.

Much could no doubt be said at this point about the history of
portraiture, but I am no expert in that field and I think I have sufficiently made my point already. Let me just make a few remarks
about the paintings of Vermeer, which serve to illustrate the kind
of approach that seems to me fruitful. These so-called 'Dutch
Interiors' typically take the following shape: a solitary individ-

ual, or pair of individuals, stands or sits in a smallish room, often strewn with artistic objects, partially bathed in soft light from a side window. The eyes are often directed towards the light, but they are not enthralled by it; some domestic business, such as writing, occupies the person's attention. The artist takes great pains with the clothes of the room's occupants, and their beauty often outshines that of the wearer. The room itself is a calm and harmonious space, beautifully fitted for human occupancy. The colours are strong but subdued, suggesting solidity and depth. Now: what is being depicted by these notably homogeneous and highly atmospheric paintings? Or, less intrusively: what might they put us in mind of that accounts for their enormous popularity and pull?

My suggestion is that these 'interiors' suggest interiors of another sort. The room is the human soul, marked by the presence of a human figure, and characterized in aesthetic terms—the hanging pictures, the sumptuous carpets, the finely fashioned clothes, the musical instruments, the organization of the room itself. The room is an enclosed space, not bright, softly defined, in which the contents are harmoniously arranged; just as the soul is apt to be conceived as an enclosed interior space, with a kind of calm translucent gloom, and furnished with an array of spiritually meaningful items. The soul is that most private of all rooms, to which one retreats from the outside world, and in which life is most intensely lived. Most suggestively of all, to my eye, the Vermeer window, which lets in a modicum of light, not an overwhelming torrent of it, is the soul's egress onto the external world: the soul is open to what lies outside it, but it maintains its quiet autonomy by filtering and reducing the light that flows in. The calm would go from the soul if it were to be engulfed by light, swamped by outside forces. The atmosphere of the room is that of a place conducive to quiet, unassuming, secularly defined virtue—the very essence of one conception of human goodness.[14] So what we are seeing in these 'interiors' of Vermeer is an

---

[14] Not the only conception, of course. I am by no means tying the ATV to this kind of quiet reclusive virtue; clearly, we need to allow for more dynamic and heroic kinds of virtue—and these may call for 'loudness' of various sorts. The beautiful soul can be spectacular, active, and strong, as well as humble, quiet and restrained. Some of the paintings of Turner, for example, suggest this kind of fiery expansive soul (to my theory-laden eye, at least).

aesthetic depiction of the soul morally conceived. And it is a soul strikingly free of religious baggage: its internal aesthetics are not those of the church or the Bible but of a man-made secular civilization. Beauty of soul is here understood in terms of a humanistic aesthetics, not an aesthetics of the transcendently supernatural (Vermeer's figures are nothing like angels). There is indeed a magic to these paintings, but it is not the magic of the traditionally miraculous; it is, if you like, the magic of the soul itself—that repository of moral worth and spiritual beauty. What is 'magical' here is human life itself, even humdrum everyday life. The soul has beauty even when going about the most mundane of business, not just when turning its face to a supernatural God and receiving His reflection. Not that the soul is invariably or necessarily a thing of beauty: there are also in these pictures hints of spiritual mediocrity or worse. But the soul is depicted as an inherently aesthetic place, just as a furnished room is: it cannot escape aesthetic, and hence moral, evaluation.

5. NABOKOV'S FORMULA

One might now ask: what is beauty such that the soul can possess it? If we knew what *kind* of property beauty is, then we would be better able to understand the thesis that the soul can be beautiful. What does it consist in for the soul to be beautiful? What does it consist in for anything to be beautiful? We must be careful with this question, however. It should not be taken as a request to reduce the notion of beauty to some other notion. We should not be trying to find non-circular necessary and sufficient conditions for something to be beautiful—or at least we should not feel obliged to undertake such a thing. Nor should we conceive of beauty as some sort of natural kind whose empirical real essence we are trying to unearth. Still less should we take the difficulty of answering the question as a reason to be sceptical about the ATV or any other theory that employs the concept of beauty. We should expect, too, that the *basis* of beauty will not be constant across all aesthetically evaluable objects; it will depend, obviously, upon the nature and composition of the object. If anything general can be said, it will be at a high level of abstraction.

Very generally, then, it seems safe to say that beauty is the property that delights our aesthetic faculties. This is not intended as an *analysis* of the concept but rather as a clear and central truth about the property of beauty. But by itself it says nothing about what delighting the aesthetic faculties might involve. Here I want to turn to some remarks of Vladimir Nabokov in the Afterword to *Lolita*, that novel of aesthetic rapture and moral depravity.[15] These remarks are striking in themselves but they also bear helpfully on our present topic. But first some comments on the scintillating novel that precedes these remarks.

Nabokov is keenly aware of the aesthetic potency of everything that concerns him as an writer, and he appreciates the attraction and repugnance that go with aesthetic evaluation. Humbert Humbert is himself a kind of aesthetic paradox, as is his passion for the nymphet: we find ourselves repelled by him and his desires but also transfixed and transported. He is the author of a sublime narrative, glittering with verbal effects and charged with dense emotion: his linguistic creation is undeniably an artistic object of rare quality. He is also described as unusually physically attractive and charming—a suave, well-dressed, cultivated, European aesthete. 'Let me repeat with quiet force: I was, and still am, despite *mes malheurs*, an exceptionally handsome male; slow-moving, tall, with soft dark hair and a gloomy but all the more seductive cast of demeanour' (25). Yet he also possesses (and conceals) a grotesque and squirming soul that hides its deformity in outward displays of artiness and civility. Speaking of his passion for nymphets, he confides:

You have to be an artist and a madman, a creature of infinite melancholy, with a bubble of hot poison in your loins and a super-voluptuous flame permanently aglow in your subtle spine (oh, how you have to cringe and hide!), in order to discern at once, by ineffable signs—the slightly feline outline of a cheekbone, the slenderness of a downy limb, and other indices which despair and shame and tears of tenderness forbid me to tabulate—the little deadly demon among the wholesome children. (17)

Inside him, indeed, Humbert is hardly a human being at all, but an alien creature squinting through treacherous eyes. He is described variously as apelike, as a spider, as a 'pentapod monster' (284), as 'just two eyes and a foot of engorged brawn'(283)— while to the outside world he is the polished and reserved

---

[15] Page references in the text are to the edition cited in the Bibliography.

gentleman that forms his disguise. He is, in fact, a marvel of aesthetic duplicity, a kind of artistic confidence-trick: 'Humbert Humbert, with thick black eyebrows and a queer accent, and a cesspoolful of rotting monsters behind his slow boyish smile' (44). It is not merely that he is grotesque within and perfectly presentable on the outside; his very spiritual repulsiveness expresses itself in the most exquisite and cultivated prose. Nabokov has, in the person of Humbert Humbert, completely bamboozled our habitual reactions to good and evil, the ugly and the beautiful. *Lolita* is a novel of aesthetic and moral trespasses.[16]

Turning now to Nabokov's general remarks on the aesthetic, he says the following: 'For me a work of fiction exists only insofar as it affords me what I shall bluntly call aesthetic bliss, that is a sense of being somehow, somewhere, connected with other states of being where art (curiosity, tenderness, kindness, ecstasy) is the norm' (314–15). He clearly means this as an account of aesthetic merit, and there is every reason to believe that he would apply it not merely to literary art but to other objects of aesthetic evaluation. Let me then paraphrase him this way: an object is beautiful if and only if it affords aesthetic bliss, and aesthetic bliss is a state of mind in which one is connected to other states of being in which art is the norm—where art involves curiosity, tenderness, kindness, and ecstasy. The beautiful object is what disposes us to experience these other-worldly states of being. In a word, it puts us into contact with certain *ideals*. There is something Platonic about Nabokov's conception here, but it is not necessary to take the talk of other states of being literally in order to see his point: we can think of these states as objects of imaginative contemplation, not as Platonic realities. The essence of the Nabokov formula is that the beautiful is what puts us in mind of the ideals listed—of a world in which these ideals are 'the norm'. We might

---

[16] This is particularly evident in the scene in which Humbert succeeds in surreptitiously masturbating against Lolita's leg while they are sitting together on the sofa: 57–61. He trespasses into Lolita's private territory, while assuring us that no breach has been made in her innocence; and he describes the sinful moment in his characteristically ecstatic prose: 'I cautiously increased the magic friction that was doing away, in an illusional, if not factual sense, with the physically irremovable, but psychologically very friable texture of the material divide (pajamas and robe) between the weight of two sunburnt legs, resting athwart my lap, and the hidden tumor of an unspeakable passion'(59). What is, in effect, child sexual abuse is rendered in terms of high poetry.

say that this is a world in which curiosity, tenderness, kindness, and ecstasy can be *taken for granted*: they constitute the prevailing laws of that world.

Now an interesting feature of this formula is that it characterizes aesthetic merit in moral terms—tenderness and kindness being moral virtues (curiosity and ecstasy *might* have a moral aspect, depending upon how they are understood). So beauty is something that puts us into contact with certain moral ideals. The beautiful object need not be *about* moral ideals, but it will cause us to take them as intentional objects of thought and feeling. The aesthetic faculty feeds into the moral faculty—recruits it. Hence the sense of moral elevation that often accompanies aesthetic delight. This becomes relevant to present concerns when we conjoin this account of beauty with our analysis of goodness. If goodness is a kind of aesthetic merit, and aesthetic merit is something that links us to certain moral ideals, then goodness is something that evokes states of mind in which moral ideals are contemplated. Nabokov's formula plus the ATV gives the result that a virtuous person makes us think of moral ideals—he or she puts us into contact with a morally ideal world. First, personal virtue delights our aesthetic faculty, by the ATV; second, our aesthetic faculty connects us to virtue in a pure undiluted form, by Nabokov's formula. When I contemplate the character of a virtuous individual in the *actual* world I am put in mind of a *possible* world in which virtue is sovereign. Aesthetic bliss (or at least appreciation) is what transports me to such a world; it is as if my mind becomes suffused with the ideals that prevail in that world. In a sense, then, I *partake* of the ideal world when I am confronted by instances of virtue in this world. And I do this precisely because of the aesthetic dimension of moral virtue. Thoughts of unalloyed and pervasive perfection are stimulated by the beautiful soul.

This is a nice result, I think, because virtue, especially exceptional virtue, *does* make us think of—even yearn for—a world in which virtue is the norm. This is one way in which the notion of heaven enters our thoughts: it is that ideal world in which morality *always* prevails. And this is a direct logical consequence of two ideas that have much intrinsic appeal—the ATV and Nabokov's formula. We thus derive a prediction that is borne out by the phenomenology of moral appreciation. The ATV takes us from morality to aesthetics, while Nabokov's formula takes us from

aesthetics to morality: the upshot is that morality leads back to itself, after taking a detour through aesthetics.

This is not a cause for disappointment, however. It does of
course follow from this that we cannot take the ATV to provide
any *reduction* or *elimination* of moral concepts in favour of aesthetic concepts, since they reappear in our account of the beautiful. But that was never the aim. What we have done is to trace out
a pattern of conceptual relations between moral and aesthetic
concepts; and the interest of the account comes in the pattern that
we find, not in any attempt to reductively explain one sort of concept in terms of the other. The moral takes us to the aesthetic and
the aesthetic takes us back to the moral; meanwhile we have
taken a trip through the soul and out to ideal Platonic worlds. So
we should not fret about the 'circularity' of the resulting picture.
Indeed, I would say that we should be *reassured* by such 'circularity', since it is generally folly to attempt any kind of wholesale reduction of one set of concepts to another.

We must not neglect evil in all this. Presumably aesthetic *demerit* has the opposite effect to that of aesthetic merit. Nabokov
says nothing about this, but the natural extension of his formula
would have it that ugliness or aesthetic demerit puts us into contact with states of being in which moral ideals are *not* the norm—
in which, instead, moral depravity is the norm. Bad art makes us
think of an anti-art world, a world in which ugliness prevails: instead of curiosity we have ignorance, instead of tenderness we
have brutality, instead of kindness we have malice, instead of ecstasy we have despair and pain: instead of contemplating a
utopia we contemplate a dystopia. Thus when we are confronted
by the ugly soul of an evil person we are transported to a world
in which evil actions and states of affairs are the controlling
norm. Our aesthetic disgust takes the form of bringing to mind
ignorance, violence, despair, and so on. Hence the peculiar feeling of depression that accompanies witnessing an aesthetically
debased would-be work of art. Again, this result is theoretically
welcome, since the evil person does make us think of what it
would be like if he were the norm; and this is predicted by the
ATV and the modified Nabokov formula. At some risk of excessive metaphor, we might think of the evil ugly soul as a sort of
microcosm of that counter-ideal world, embodying within it the
world we fear might become actual. We cannot contemplate an

evil individual without thinking of an all-too-close possible world in which his evil is magnified a thousand times. This is one reason evil people are so terrifying and disturbing: they represent a mere pocket of some larger potential evil; their existence seems like a foretaste of hell. Dystopian works of art draw upon this tendency, conjuring the evil possible world that is implicit in the localized evils we witness in the actual world.

What also emerges from the Nabokov formula is that the supposition of a beautiful yet vicious soul receives another rebuff. For if beauty puts us into contact with moral ideals, then it is hard to see how this could be so for the alleged case of the beautiful but evil soul: that would have to mean that we could be put into contact with ideal goodness by an object that was intrinsically *bad*. The evil of the person would evoke thoughts of badness, while his alleged spiritual beauty would, by Nabokov's formula, makes us think of moral goodness. One and the same thing would inspire exactly opposite moral reactions. To put it mildly, the resulting state of mind would be jarring and unsustainable. So the Nabokov formula underwrites the convergence we are insisting upon.

6. SOME CONSEQUENCES OF THE THEORY

The idea of the soul's being, or becoming, *visible* holds great fascination for us. This is the conceit upon which *The Picture of Dorian Gray* so strikingly fixes. What would it be like if we could literally see into each other's, and our own, soul? We suppose this to be one of God's special prerogatives: He really can *see* the condition of a soul. So we think we can imagine what it would be for the soul to be visible. Pressed to give content to this (dubiously intelligible) idea, we are apt to picture the soul by means of the human face, since this is the part of the body that most delicately expresses what goes on in the mind. For the soul to be visible, then, would be for it to have a face of its own, distinct from the external physical face. The question then is what such a face would look like.

Since the soul is the seat of virtue and vice, its face must present its moral state. In principle, any visual feature could do this—colour, size—but in fact we seize upon aesthetic qualities as representative of virtue. The face of the good soul is visually beautiful, that of the bad soul visually ugly. Religious iconography abounds in such depictions—as with pictures of Jesus Christ and of the devil. What is going on here is this: the idea of beauty of soul is transmuted into a visual representation, this being the aesthetic sense that we tend to gravitate towards. The fact that we choose an aesthetic representation of the moral state of a soul when we render it visible shows that we were *already* conceiving of it in aesthetic terms. Why is the face of the soul seen as beautiful or ugly? Because the goodness or evil of the soul *is* an aesthetic matter. How else could one convincingly represent virtue in a visible embodiment of the soul *except* by aesthetic means? Logically one could, say by using red for good and blue for evil, but in fact nothing else strikes us as naturally suited to the concept of virtue we have. Visible virtue *has* to be represented aesthetically, because that is the way we think of the *in*visible beauty of the soul. In other words, the use of the visual beauty or ugliness of a face to represent the moral state of a soul made visible is *explained* by the fact that we already conceive of the virtuous soul in aesthetic terms.

Rendering the soul in visual form would effect a transformation in moral epistemology. Normally, our knowledge of someone's moral state, including our own, is frustratingly indirect and uncertain. We cannot easily *tell* whether someone has a virtuous character, even in our own case. Large errors of trust can be made because of this indirectness and uncertainty. Dorian's portrait, by contrast, has the remarkable power to reveal immediately and infallibly his moral condition. The uglier the portrait looks, the more depraved he is—no room for debate. The attraction of the visible soul, as an imaginative fancy, is thus to hold out the possibility of surer ethical knowledge than we possess, and beauty is the means by which such knowledge can be conveyed. As things are—and as things metaphysically must be—the beauty of a soul is not open to instant and certain sensory assessment; but, craving surer access to virtue, we readily fall in with the idea of a form of beauty that yields itself up instantly to the eye. We deeply want beauty of soul to be part of the *given*, so that the dangers of error are eliminated.[17] That we try, if only in imagination,

---

[17] At the same time, we fear such moral exposure—and not just in our own

to remove our epistemological quandaries by such means, shows that we are tacitly conceiving of virtue according to the ATV.

We not only admire and esteem virtue, while deprecating vice; we also love and cherish virtue, while hating and despising vice. In much moral philosophy you would think that we go around merely approving and disapproving of things—*judging* right and wrong. But of course it is a much more visceral affair than that; our passions are engaged. Emotivism was no doubt mistaken as a theory of moral judgement, but it was not wrong in supposing that morality recruits our affective faculties. Evil repels us; goodness attracts us. The ideas of 'love of virtue' and 'hatred of evil' are part of the basic phenomenology of moral experience. We might wonder why this should be: why isn't morality as dispassionate a subject as physics or history? The ATV suggests an answer: because beauty and ugliness also excite such feelings—we are attracted to the beautiful and shun the ugly. (I do not say that this is always a good thing, especially when it comes to the human face and figure—but it is a fact.) Thus we can explain our affective attitudes towards virtue and vice by noting their alliances with the aesthetic. When we love the virtuous person we are responding to his inner beauty, somewhat as we do to a work of art; and similarly for our hatred of the evil person. These affective associations are not proof of 'non-cognitivism' about moral judgement; they are indications that the moral and the aesthetic intersect. The beautiful is what gives delight, and we take delight in the virtuous person; the ATV explains this coincidence.

Moral pride is often regarded as uniquely sinful. This is no doubt exaggerated, the result of a slave mentality that insists upon modesty at any price and regardless of the facts. Still, there is something peculiarly distasteful about preening oneself on one's virtue; a person who does so strikes us as contemptible, even morally paradoxical. Does he not expunge his own moral perfection precisely by celebrating it? But why do we respond in this way to moral pride? Why isn't it just like preening oneself on one's athletic or intellectual abilities—no better, no worse? Why is moral self-glorification a vice set apart? The ATV has an answer: because it is a form of narcissism. The physically beautiful

case. Would we all be happier if we each had our own soul-portrait up in the attic, just like Dorian Gray? It would certainly have an enormous impact on the conduct of our lives, morally speaking.

person may succumb to vanity, staring raptly in the mirror and parading his looks; the spiritually beautiful person runs a comparable risk, gazing upon her own inner beauty in an attitude of narcissism. When I judge that I am virtuous I am judging that I am beautiful of soul, and this puts me in peril of spiritual narcissism. Moral pride as a vice is thus a special case of narcissism as a vice. Possessing inner beauty puts me at risk of being too much in love with myself, too attracted to my own soul. As I am attracted to the moral beauty of others, so I may become fixated on my own moral beauty. But since narcissism is a vice, this will compromise such moral beauty as I possess.[18] Hence the paradoxical position of the morally prideful. Self-love is the moral pitfall and temptation of the beautiful soul: that inward-looking, solipsistic, entrancement with one's own radiant being. The only sure cure for it is a resolute refusal to allow one's attention to be focused on one's own inner moral workings. The beautiful soul must have its gaze directed firmly outward, to the world of action and other people.

If virtue is beauty, and beauty produces aesthetic pleasure, then the virtuous person should be the occasion of aesthetic pleasure. We derive aesthetic pleasure from works of art and formations of nature, among other things, so too should we derive aesthetic pleasure from a beautiful soul. The ATV thus predicts that virtue will cause the kind of pleasure in us that all beauty causes. But does it? It might be argued that there are counterexamples to such a general claim: take the self-denying austere disciplinarian—the stereotypical Victorian kill-joy. *He* produces no aesthetic pleasure in us, surely, but is he not a model of rectitude? Such an example is not easy to evaluate without further details, but the outlines of an answer are not far to seek. He *may* be an example of stripped-down, simple, functional aesthetic quality—the Mission chair of the moral universe. He has the ascetic virtues and so possesses a soul that mirrors aesthetically those traits. But he may also be a cruel and unforgiving figure, much given to the

---

[18] It is not easy to say exactly *why* narcissism is a vice, though the intuition is strong. It can hardly be simply that it involves excessive flattery of the self. I think it has more to do with the way it misdirects love: the narcissist loves herself at the expense of loving others. She is devoted to herself alone. She is a faithful onanist, reflexively monogamous in her passions. Compare Woody Allen's famous remark: 'Don't knock masturbation—it's having sex with someone I love!'

lash, and intolerant of others. In that case he indeed gives no aesthetic pleasure, but then he is also not rightly styled virtuous (though he may be so described by the erroneous standards of his society). In either case, he is no counterexample to the ATV.

It does seem to me that I derive aesthetic pleasure from the company of people I judge to be virtuous, and that others (as we revealingly say) 'get up my nose'. One reason we like to spend time with virtuous people is for the aesthetic pleasure they provide, not merely for the good turns they may do us.[19] There is much more of this in social interchange than seems commonly recognized: we seek beauty in all its forms, and virtue is one of them. Among the most troubling people to know are those who have some aesthetic qualities in abundance but are lacking in the moral kind: you don't know whether to be attracted or repelled, to stay or to go. It is as if you can derive aesthetic pleasure of one kind from them only by being willing to put up with some aesthetic repugnance. The typical outcome is cognitive dissonance and a consequent refusal to accept their moral ugliness, despite the plain facts. For the sake of the face you deny the soul. Much self-delusion can result from this and eventual disillusionment on a grand scale. Physically beautiful people are dangerous for precisely this reason, to themselves as well as others: we are prone to overlook their moral failings, so that nothing is done to curb them. Here is Reid on the subject: 'It cannot indeed be denied, that the expression of a fine countenance may be unnaturally disjoined from the amiable qualities which it naturally expresses: but we presume the contrary, till we have a clear evidence; and even then, we pay homage to the expression, as we do to the throne when it happens to be unworthily filled' (806). Such aesthetically bifurcated individuals can be sources of much pain and strife, sometimes despite themselves. In some cases, of course, they consciously exploit their power to deflect moral disapproval and get away with murder. In this respect, at least, it is easier for the plain to be good, because they are not lulled into moral laziness. The externally beautiful can expect love no matter how ghastly they are at heart. They are a kind of simulacrum

---

[19] Remember that I am not taking virtue to be always of the stolid, dull variety. Bravery, imagination, and individuality can also constitute a virtuous character— and I would say of the most attractive kind. Certainly, mindless conformity is no part of a proper conception of virtue.

of goodness, a visual illusion of virtue. That is not to say that they cannot be virtuous, of course—just that they will present a superficial impression of virtue no matter what. Like Dorian Gray, they will automatically inspire love and trust, even while their soul is as hideous as may be.

7. VIRTUE AND ART

Is beauty of soul an achievement or a natural fact? Do we create our own inner beauty, as an artist creates a work of art, or does nature provide us with an attractive or repellent soul? According to the ATV, that question is the same as the question whether we make our own virtue. It is not my purpose here to argue for any particular answer to this question, only to indicate what it *means* if the ATV is true. How should we think about the genesis of virtue if virtue is inner beauty? If virtue is outside our intentional control, being a matter of genetic determination, then our inner beauty has the same kind of genesis as our physical beauty. It is a natural phenomenon to whose upkeep we can contribute but whose essential lineaments are not subject to the will. For the record, I side with traditional wisdom in believing that this cannot be the whole story of the formation of moral character. We are masters of our moral destiny, at least to some degree, which means that we create our own inner beauty or the lack of it. Then the point I want to make is that this is to construct a work of art in a quite literal sense—the moral life *is* a sort of artistic life. And I use the word 'art' here in both of its main senses: as something that requires skill (artifice) and not merely the deliverances of nature; and as something that has aesthetic qualities. The effort to be a good person is an artistic project in these two senses; we are architects of the soul.

This perspective has two sorts of bearing on the conduct of moral life—one regarding method, the other motivation. What 'techniques' should be adopted in the pursuit of virtue? I hope I shall not be accused of misplaced aestheticism if I suggest that the techniques of the artist are not out of place here. The artist lavishes his full attention on his construction, caring about both the details and the overall form of the final product; he also keeps his eye firmly on reality, to which his product must stand in some intelligible relation. The artist is above all concerned to create something with inner integrity and merit, that will survive the test of time, that will bring delight to others. All these aims are appropriate to the creation of virtue, *mutatis mutandis*: it too requires the fullest commitment of one's highest faculties, a willed perfectionism about what is created. The methods by which beauty is invested in an artistic object have their necessary counterparts in the production of a beautiful soul. The refusal to compromise or conform is an essential ingredient in both sorts of endeavour. Perhaps due recognition of this commonality might help focus our efforts in the moral sphere. It also suggests that even the most philistine among us cannot escape at least one artistic project (assuming a commitment to moral virtue).

As to motivation, we can be brief. It is often asked why we should be moral. If the analogy to the artist is appropriate, we have a ready answer: in order to increase the amount of beauty in the world. Beauty is valuable, virtue is beauty, so virtue is valuable. Not only that: the beauty created is beauty in oneself; so an additional motive is that of increasing one's *own* beauty. And surely we all want to do *that*. To say this is not say that morality cannot also be its own motivation; but to those who find such a view too bleakly austere there is the pull of the beautiful to fall back on. The project of virtue is thus motivationally overdetermined.[20]

A quite different question about the relation between virtue and art is this: how does the beauty of one's surroundings bear upon one's moral state? It is sometimes said that virtue is encouraged by exposure to beautiful things and vice encouraged by exposure to ugly things. Bad architecture, say, will promote bad character; good music will instil nobility. Though surely by no means rigidly reliable, there does seem to be something in this

---

[20] Norton, in *The Beautiful Soul*, observes that the idea of moral beauty was regarded at its outset as an alternative to a religiously based motivation for morality: 55–79. Instead of fear of hell and yearning for heaven being the reason to be moral, the motivation was now to be found in the ideal of self-perfection. Thus religious moralists were deeply opposed to the idea of an aesthetic morality—and for good reason, given their conception of human moral motivation. (My own view is that the search for moral motivation outside the dictates of morality itself is misguided.)

supposed correlation. Bad art can be not just an effect of moral shoddiness but also a cause of it. At any rate, let us go along with this familiar idea in order to see what light the ATV might shed on it. What might be the *mechanism* connecting outer art to inner virtue? Again, the ATV has an answer. Human beings are prone to imitation, to forming themselves after the style of what they observe. We laugh when others laugh, we yawn when they do, we dress in fashion, we speak with the same accent as those around us. It is clearly part of human learning to imitate others— sometimes to very bad effect, as we all know. It is a tendency we innately possess: we are constitutionally inclined to become like what we observe around us. Nor is there any reason to think this tendency limited to the imitation of other *people*; we might well find that the *products* of people are also objects of imitation. Suppose then that you are surrounded by beautiful well-designed objects, things that produce aesthetic pleasure. Then you will be inclined to mimic those things in your own person. You might dress and move and speak more beautifully if your place of habitation is itself beautiful. But you might also take the beauty further inward, internalizing it: you might become more beautiful in your soul. But this, by the ATV, *is* virtue; so the process of aesthetic imitation will result in the growth of virtue. Beautiful surroundings will foster moral virtue, by means of an intelligible psychological mechanism. And of course the same mechanism will operate to convert ugly surroundings into viciousness of character, as the outer ugliness becomes internalized.

The quality of a society's architecture, therefore, will matter to the morality of the community; it will tend to be absorbed into the inner aesthetics of the community's members by the method of mimicry. And the same goes for design of all kinds. So the better a society's taste in outer things, the better placed it will be to promote virtue. Quality of culture promotes goodness of character, as well as reflecting it. If this is right, then programmes of social improvement need to take into account both the aesthetic quality of the environment and the aesthetic taste of those living in it. Moral education won't be just a matter of direct moral instruction, or a system of rewards and punishments; it will involve the wider question of the aesthetic quality of the culture. We cannot treat these as wholly unrelated areas. Aesthetic pollution has a tendency to lead to moral pollution, because morality is bound up with the aesthetic. The modern city can be a dangerous place, in terms of the quality of one's inner architecture. The phrase 'mean streets', used to name a well-known film about urban violence and moral decay, perfectly fuses the twin ideas of inner and outer architectural ugliness.[21]

Let me end this discussion of the beautiful soul with a more general point: that aesthetic notions have a far broader application than is sometimes supposed. There is a tendency for people to think of the aesthetic in much too narrow terms, as if it included only what is to be found in museums and art galleries, along with natural landscapes. But the aesthetic permeates almost every experience a human being has, and at many levels. We are aesthetic beings through and through; we apprehend the world through aesthetic eyes. Not only are other people perceived aesthetically, so are animals of other species. Not only are buildings and sculptures aesthetic objects, so are kitchen knives and screwdrivers and stereo systems. Speech acts have aesthetic properties. Ideas and thoughts do too. It is hard to name anything that lacks an aesthetic dimension, positive or negative. Panaestheticism is the indicated doctrine. In this chapter I have argued that the domain of the aesthetic includes people's inner lives—that characters can be beautiful or ugly. Perhaps this idea will seem all but inevitable once the full extent of the aesthetic is recognized. For why should the mind alone be thought incapable of aesthetic description? It would be amazing if the mind *lacked* aesthetic properties (the brain certainly has them). And once this is acknowledged, the connection with morality is a natural next step. Seen in this light, the ATV can seem like a virtual truism, not an outlandish piece of poetic metaphysics.

I can think of only one reason why the idea of beauty of soul might be resisted (irrespective of its connection with morality). It is a deep metaphysical reason: namely, that in some sense we do not know what it would *be* for the mind to have aesthetic properties, since we do not know what kind of thing the mind *is*. Is it material or immaterial or some other unknown type of thing? What kind of theory governs its operations? What are its elements and modes of combination? The mind is a mystery, a

[21] *Mean Streets*, directed by Martin Scorcese, 1973.

region of deep ignorance.[22] And because we don't know what kind of thing the mind is, we are naturally puzzled about what it means to ascribe aesthetic properties to it. To have a clear conception of what beauty of mind might be we need a conception of the *nature* of what is thus beautiful—but that is precisely what we lack. Granted, we *talk* as if the mind has aesthetic properties, but we cannot explicate what this ultimately consists in. In the case of a painting, say, we have paint marks on canvas as the medium of aesthetic quality; but what is the medium of *mental* beauty? What type of 'material' is configured into what we have been calling a beautiful soul?

These perplexities are not groundless, but they should not detach us from the concept of mental beauty. We can know that the mind has certain characteristics without having a theory of its nature. Our entire knowledge of the mind is premised on this possibility. We know, for example, that human minds house beliefs and desires and sensations without knowing what *constitutes* these things. What we know now is that *whatever* the mind turns out to be it will have a nature that permits it to have aesthetic attributes—since it manifestly *has* such attributes. Still, it is perhaps natural that the metaphysical problems of mind should infect our thinking about the notion of mental beauty. This latter concept will inherit the mystery that attaches to the mind considered generally. But this mystery is no more reason to reject the concept of mental beauty than it is a reason to reject the very existence of the mind.[23]

---

[22] I happen to believe that the mystery is terminal—see McGinn, *The Problem of Consciousness*. At any rate, it is a current mystery, by almost anyone's standards. Since virtue is inseparable from being a conscious subject, mental beauty will necessarily involve consciousness; so the mystery of consciousness is bound to spill over to the notion of mental beauty. More precisely, we do not know the *constitution* of the bearer of mental (and hence moral) beauty, namely, the conscious subject.

[23] It might be a reason—yet another one—for denying the reducibility of the mental to the physical, since the aesthetic properties of the mind are not mirrored in the aesthetic properties of the brain. The brain of even the most beautiful soul is pretty unpleasant to look at! Thus there must be more to the mind than the brain as currently conceived.

6

The Picture: Dorian Gray

1. ART AND SIN

Art is responsive to beauty. Often enough, it becomes beautiful by depicting the beautiful. But what is its relation to sin? Can art make beauty out of sin, or is sin itself a form of ugliness? What are the aesthetic powers of sin? And which is the stronger, art or morality? How should we conduct our lives with respect to art and beauty? Is it possible to love beauty too much? Can life be made into art? At what moral cost? These are some the themes addressed in Oscar Wilde's *The Picture of Dorian Gray*.[1] On the surface, the book is a gothic melodrama, a horror story, featuring murder, blackmail, Satanic pacts, the supernatural—along with much witty dialogue, and some homosexual hints. But it is also a complex meditation on the relations between art and morality, especially as these are embedded in human life. In this chapter, I shall attempt to tease out the conceptual apparatus with which Wilde operates in the book, and indicate what lessons it draws. I shall also put forward some specific interpretative theses about the structure of the story.

The idea of a duality of aesthetic levels to human life, inner and outer, is a central tenet of *Dorian Gray*. The book explores the consequences of a radical dissociation of the two levels, which are normally linked in ordinary mortal life—especially the moral consequences of such a dissociation. Dorian is an experiment in aesthetic splitting. Extreme ugliness within is coupled with striking exterior beauty. The inner ugliness is held to be equivalent to moral depravity of character, so that Dorian's face and figure act as a mask to conceal his moral corruption. His sins are opaque to

---

[1] Page references in the text are to the edition cited in the Bibliography. I shall assume some familiarity with the story.

those around him, not being etched on his features, and he can exploit the illusion of moral virtue his appearance projects. His sinful self makes not the slightest mark on his body, even as his soul becomes ever more repulsive. He can gaze in secret upon the terrible face of his soul, while others are hypnotized by his exterior beauty into believing him virtuous. He works like a walking visual illusion of virtue that the viewer cannot shake off, even when he knows the truth. The power of the aesthetic both to conceal and express evil is thus presented in an extreme and exemplary form. Dorian Gray is emblematic of all of us.

There are three main characters in Wilde's tale of friendship, influence, and fate: Basil Hallward, a gifted painter; Lord Henry Wotton, a brilliant talker; and Dorian Gray, a naturally beautiful young man. Each of them is passionately attached to beauty, in one way or another. The book itself is drenched in ecstatic descriptions of sensuous beauty ('the gleam of the honey-sweet and honey-coloured blossoms of a laburnum, whose tremulous branches seemed hardly able to bear the burden of a beauty so flame-like as theirs' (23), and so on). The story opens with Basil having just finished a remarkable life-sized portrait of Dorian, who has inspired and disturbed him. Basil fears that he has put too much of himself into his picture, that he has bared his idolatrous soul in it, and resolves never to show it. He tells us that 'every portrait that is painted with feeling is a portrait of the artist, not of the sitter. The sitter is merely the accident, the occasion. It is not he who is revealed by the painter; it is rather the painter who, on the coloured canvas, reveals himself. The reason I will not exhibit this picture is that I am afraid that I have shown in it the secret of my own soul' (27). Thus the painting is already imbued with the seeds of its later animism—it has absorbed some of its maker's soul. Presumably this is why it is so strangely responsive to Dorian's later plea. It will in due course come to reveal the secret of the sitter's soul; for now, it reveals that of the artist. It is the amalgam of the two that gives the portrait its miraculous power. Basil resolves to give it to Dorian for his eyes only, so that the world will not know of the influence Dorian has exercised over him. Since he has lost his soul to Dorian, he makes a gift to the thief of what has been taken from him. Dorian has reshaped his art; it remains now for Dorian to be reshaped by it.

Lord Henry has not yet met Dorian, but he soon does, against

Basil's wishes, and, like Basil, he is immediately struck by Dorian's personal beauty and charm. 'There was something in his face that made one trust him at once. All the candour of youth was there, as well as all youth's passionate purity. One felt that he had kept himself unspotted from the world. No wonder Basil Hallward worshipped him' (39). From the first, Henry sets out to influence Dorian's thoughts and feelings by propounding, with his 'beautiful voice' (40), a view of morality that sets it below art and regards traditional virtue as mere cowardice. 'Conscience and cowardice are really the same things, Basil. Conscience is the trade-name of the firm. That is all' (29). He encourages Dorian, in that 'low, musical voice' (41) of his, to celebrate his exceptional looks and to cast off the conventional morality that encumbers his growth. Dorian is told to return to the 'Hellenic ideal' (41) of free expression, that only spiritual sickness and misery can result from suppressing his natural impulses. No more helping the poor of the East End—Dorian must attend to his own life and its possibilities. While he is being exposed to these dangerously attractive ideas, Dorian gazes at his portrait for the first time. He is greatly struck by his likeness in the picture, seeing his own beauty reflected in the medium of art, and this reinforces the accompanying advice from Henry to take his own beauty more seriously. He begins, at this point, to see himself *as* a work of art. He feels the duties of an artist towards his own person. When Henry reminds him of the transience of youth, and hence beauty, observing that all too soon he will no longer look as he does now, he sends Dorian into a kind of proleptic despair. All that is most valuable and sublime in him will be expunged by time. 'The life that was to make his soul would mar his body. He would become dreadful, hideous and uncouth' (49). From being an inspiration to art, he will become the ugliness from which art offers us escape. The painting has the aesthetic permanence that his mortality denies him. Basil and Henry working together make him see that.

Thus Dorian has already become a vector for two lines of influence from his creatively gifted friends: a visual influence from Basil in the form of a superlative work of art and the idolatry it contains; and a discursive moral influence from the eloquent, witty, and penetrating Henry. Basil creates the opportunity for Henry to seize hold of Dorian's soul and make him value his own beauty above all else. The work of art is the stimulus towards Dorian's self-celebration and eventual moral decline. As the novel progresses, this pair of co-operating forces comes more and more to dominate Dorian, so that he becomes simply the confluence of two aesthetic influences (he begins with little personality of his own). He becomes, in effect, the handiwork of two creative geniuses, one in the realm of painting, the other in the realm of conversation. He is their joint artistic creation, a work of their respective arts. He is thus thoroughly suffused with art and artifice. Indeed, as I shall be arguing, he *is* a work of art.

This is almost literally true in the case of Basil's influence, because it is the painting, assisted by Henry's paean to youth and beauty, that causes Dorian to make his transforming pact with the devil: that he should take the place of the painting and remain beautiful and unchanged, while it bears the marks of time and deed.

'How sad it is!' murmured Dorian Gray, with his eyes still fixed upon his own portrait. 'How sad it is! I shall grow old, and horrible, and dreadful. But this picture will remain always young. It will never be older than this particular day of June . . . If it were only the other way! If it were I who was to be always young, and the picture that was to grow old! For that—for that—I would give everything. Yes, there is nothing in the whole world I would not give! I would give my soul for that!' (49)

So it is the existence of Basil's painting that enables Dorian to stay exactly as he is, no matter how much time goes by and how many sins he commits. Basil's artistic idolatry is what permits Dorian to become the timeless aesthetic object that the story chiefly concerns. It is his work that enables, and incites, Dorian to change places with the picture, thus acquiring its properties. In comparison, Henry's influence is merely facilitatory. Not that there is any malicious impulse behind Basil's work: the evil effects of his art stem from the highest aesthetic intentions and abilities. As he remarks: 'Your rank and wealth, Harry; my brains, such as they are—my art, whatever it may be worth; Dorian Gray's good looks—we shall all suffer for what the gods have given us, suffer terribly' (25–6). The story deals with the tragic consequences of actions motivated by high aesthetic ideals and exceptional talent.

Lord Henry's influence consists in setting up an opposition between art and morality and urging that art is the superior form of value. Dorian then enacts this philosophy in his own life. In making his fateful pact, he chooses to insulate himself from morality, to remove himself from its visible verdicts, by shifting its natural operations onto the canvas; he can then live as if aesthetic value were all that matters. By forgetfulness and aesthetic distraction he protects himself from consciousness of his own sin, and the portrait is left to bear all the corporeal marks that would serve to remind him of moral reality. He seeks to become the kind of thing with respect to which moral appraisal is *irrelevant*. In effect, he tries to attain the status ascribed to art in the aphorisms that preface the novel. 'There is no such thing as a moral or an immoral book. Books are well-written, or badly written. That is all.' 'No artist has ethical sympathies. An ethical sympathy in an artist is an unpardonable mannerism of style.' 'Vice and virtue are to the artist materials for an art' (21). (Whether Wilde's own book is as morally neutral as these dicta suggest, is a question to which we shall return.) What Dorian does is to push aestheticism to its limits, making an art of his life, even its immoral aspects. He converts every facet of life, even death, into something aesthetic. Sin is merely an opportunity for artistic expression. Instead of requiring the work of art to be subject to ethical evaluation, Dorian makes art superordinate over ethics, so that acts and events are judged solely by their aesthetic qualities. When Sibyl Vane, an actress, kills herself because of Dorian's callous desertion of her, his response, abetted by Lord Henry, is to see her suicide as but a beautiful moment in a finely wrought tragic work. He says: 'I admit that this thing that has happened does not affect me as it should. It seems to me simply like a wonderful ending to a wonderful play. It has all the terrible beauty of a Greek tragedy, a tragedy in which I took a great part, but by which I have not been wounded' (130). Since he remains aesthetically untarnished, he feels able to construe his actions and their effects as themselves beautiful. He is an aesthetically enclosed being in whom the moral sense has been supplanted by the aesthetic sense. There is no more sin in him than in a beautiful painting in which sin has been merely depicted. So long as sin is aesthetically expressed, there can be no objection to it. Art cancels sin by appropriating it.

2. PICTURE AND PERSON

I have said that Dorian is an artistic product; now I want to make the more specific suggestion that, as a result of his pact with the devil, he is transformed *into* a picture. He switches roles with the original canvas. Dorian becomes numerically identical with the picture of Dorian, a self-referential art work. According to this suggestion, then, he becomes a work of art in a quite literal sense. Where the canvas once depicted him, he now depicts the person manifest in the canvas. What happens when the pact is made is that the picture shifts location, from the pigments on the canvas to Dorian's flesh-and-blood body. Thus, since Dorian himself does not change with time, though the image on the canvas does, as his soul mutates morally, the *picture* of Dorian stays constant, as a work of art should. It is not that the original depiction goes out of existence or sacrifices the attribute of changelessness (which, by the book's standards, disqualifies it from being a work of art); rather, it takes up residence in Dorian's body. If the picture had remained on the canvas and Dorian had altered and aged, then it would also have stayed constant, having the immortality that the book assigns to art; but instead the picture retains its immortality, *despite* the alterations in the canvas, by taking up a new habitation, in the body of its erstwhile object. The work of art is thus conserved, but it is conserved in a living breathing being. Dorian does not then merely live his life *as if* he is a work of art; he *is* a work of art—a representation, an image. That, I suggest, is the central conceit of the book, the literal conflation of person and picture, of life and art. Dorian is his own portrait, the ultimate absorption of the world into its artistic representation. He makes his life into art precisely by supernaturally changing his status from mortal being to immortal art object. The pact is really an act of metamorphosis from person to picture. He does exactly what Lord Henry recommends, but far more literally than Henry could ever have imagined. He has 'passed . . . into the sphere of art' (139), to appropriate the phrase Dorian himself employs to describe the death of Sibyl. As she is now nothing but the great Shakespearean heroines she portrayed so marvellously, so he becomes the wonderful work of art Basil Hallward idolatrously painted. She owes her only real existence to a playwright, he to a painter.

I am not saying that this identification is directly and wood-enly stated in the text, but I think it is Wilde's intention all the same. It is an interpretation that is particularly relevant to the final scene of the book, which otherwise is puzzling and peculiar. This is a scene that superficially seems to contradict the interpre-tation I favour, but a close look at it actually bears out what I am suggesting. Before I turn to this, however, let me note how my suggestion comports with other elements of the story.

When the canvas first begins to show signs of Dorian's moral decline, by assuming a look of cruelty around the mouth, he has it transferred to the attic in which, significantly, he spent much of his boyhood, before the pact was ever made. Here his soul is seen to undergo the transformations that reflect its owner's life—it shows grotesque marks of age and sin. It changes predictably from beautiful to hideous, while Dorian remains eternally youth-ful and innocent-seeming. The canvas is thus the living, changing thing, expressive of a spirit, while he is fixed and immutable, mummified almost. Dorian's soul is there in the attic, if any-where, and thus has a claim to carrying his identity. The face on the canvas is described as grinning, as leering, as inciting Dorian to action, just as a person might do; while we imagine the three-dimensional Dorian as expressionless and facially immobile, like a picture that has escaped from a gallery.[2] The properties of the canvas, on the other hand, become quite uncharacteristic of a work of art. In order for Dorian to take on the changelessness of a work of art, which is what the pact requires, his soul must depart his body, taking up another location; but then *he* is no longer where his body is. He cannot keep his soul with him *and* have the immortality of art. This is the precise effect the portrait originally had on him—to make him lose his soul, to make him give it up. It duly migrates, while he freezes into a mere statue (though a mo-bile plastic one). Thus, when Basil comes to confront Dorian about the rumours circulating around his name, Dorian says: 'I shall show you my soul. You shall see the thing that you fancy only God can see' (186)—speaking of the thing in the attic. And, when Basil is made witness to Dorian's secret, we read that 'it

---

[2] This is how Dorian is played by Hurd Hatfield in the film version of the novel, often with a frame of some sort placed behind his head: *The Picture of Dorian Gray*, directed by Albert Lewin, 1945.

was Dorian Gray's own face he was looking at! . . . Yes, it was Dorian himself' (189). Meanwhile Dorian is described as 'leaning against the mantleshelf' (189), as impassive as a picture. He remarks, of the canvas, 'It is the face of my soul' (190), thus transferring ownership of his identity to the painting. Plainly, then, there has been a reassignment of status as between person and picture. And this is the logical limit of the aesthete's approach to life, which is the central theme of the book—actual subsumption in the category of art. Imagined cinematically, we might visualize this as the figure in the portrait literally stepping out from the canvas and merging into Dorian's body, as his soul seeps out from his body and into the canvas. He is, thereafter, a kind of special effect—an artistic contrivance. Dorian's picture is not hidden in the attic, after all; it accompanies him wherever he goes.

Let us now look at the denouement. Toward the end of the book Dorian undertakes to redeem himself. He says to Henry: 'The soul is a terrible reality. It can be bought, and sold, and bartered away. It can be poisoned, or made perfect. There is a soul in each one of us. I know it' (252). His first good act, as he thinks, is to spare the reputation of Hetty Merton, a girl with whom he has been conducting an affair, by telling her it is over. Henry responds: 'My dear boy, you are really beginning to moralize. You will soon be going about like the converted, and the revivalist, warning people against all the sins of which you have grown tired. You are much too delightful to do that. Besides, it is no use. You and I are what we are, and will be what we will be' (257). But Dorian is determined to salvage his soul:

He felt a wild longing for the unstained purity of his boyhood—his rose-white boyhood, as Lord Henry had once called it. He knew that he had tarnished himself, filled his mind with corruption, and given horror to his fancy; that he had been an evil influence to others, and had experienced a terrible joy in being so; and that, of the lives that had crossed his own, it had been the fairest and most full of promise that he had brought to shame. But was it all irretrievable? Was there no hope for him? (259)

The answer, it turns out, and as Henry foretells, is that there is indeed no hope for him. He cannot change—it is too late for that now. Despite what he took to be a good act, the painting in the attic advises him otherwise, and it is an infallible authority on his moral condition. He sees no change in the direction of virtue, but only

that in the eyes there was a look of cunning, and in the mouth the curved wrinkle of the hypocrite. The thing was still loathsome—more loathsome, if possible, than before—and the scarlet dew that spotted the hand seemed brighter, and more like blood newly spilt . . . Through vanity he had spared her. In hypocrisy he had worn the mask of goodness. For curiosity's sake he had tried the denial of self. He recognised that now. (261–2)

In other words, his soul is by now so sunk in depravity, so comprehensively stained, that he is quite incapable of summoning a good act or motive; there is nothing good *left* in him. He wants to be good—or at least it seems to him that he does—but he is no longer able to be; his soul is irretrievably lost. He did, after all, offer his soul to the devil, and the devil is not about to give it back to him. Accordingly, he has no escape from evil save one—to put an end to his life. That is the predicament in which he now finds himself.

This is the immediate background to the final decisive scene, and it is important to keep it in mind in interpreting what happens in that scene. Seeing the knife with which he had earlier murdered Basil, he resolves to destroy the artist's creation:

As it had killed the painter, so it would kill the painter's work, and all that that meant. It would kill the past, and when that was dead he would be free. It would kill this monstrous soul-life, and, without its hideous warnings, he would be at peace. He seized the thing, and stabbed the picture with it. There was a cry heard, and a crash. The cry was so horrible in its agony that the frightened servants woke, and crept out of their rooms. (263)

What precisely is going on in this highly abbreviated and remote description? On a superficial reading of the text, what happens is that Dorian decides to destroy the canvas so that it will no longer remind him of the moral monster he has become. He will then live on, evilly, without this evidence of his evil, for his eyes or the prying eyes of others. He therefore plunges the knife into the canvas, presumably with the intention of ripping it to shreds. A cry and crash are heard from below, as the stabbed painting falls to the floor, as heavy as a man, emitting a death cry. Dorian, we

presume, stands over it, gloating, knife in hand. So we might for-
givably suppose from the words we are given.

When the servants arrive, however, the scene is otherwise
than we might expect. The final short paragraph reads:

When they entered they found, hanging on the wall, a splendid portrait
of their master as they had last seen him, in all the wonder of his exquisite youth and beauty. Lying on the floor was a dead man, in evening
dress, with a knife in his heart. He was withered, wrinkled, and loathsome of visage. It was not till they had examined the rings that they
recognised who it was. (264)

Contrary to expectation, the canvas is unripped, still hanging,
and has resumed its original condition; while Dorian lies on the
floor, a knife in his heart, his face unrecognizable because it has
assumed the appearance of the last hideous stages of the painting. What *happened* up there? We are not made witness to it; so we
must conjecture. Superficially, Dorian is mysteriously killed, not
as a result of his own intention, but by courtesy of a weird supernatural intrusion in which God (as it might be) decides to punish
him for his evil acts. Dorian's intention was to destroy the painting, not himself, but some outside force saw to it that he was destroyed instead. From the act of stabbing the painting the knife
miraculously turns from the canvas somehow and finds its way
into his heart. The slashing of the canvas has also been magically
reversed, so that it is now intact. It cannot be that he somehow
missed the canvas as the supernatural force took effect, since we
are told definitively that 'he stabbed the picture'. The two visages
are then relocated, the pact having been broken by Dorian's decision to destroy the painting. The crash then came from him, not
from the painting, and presumably the cry was also his as the
knife jumped from the canvas into his heart, no doubt to his ap-
palled astonishment. It was all the result of a *deus ex machina*—
the standard fallback of the gothic horror story.

This is certainly the natural way to read the text, despite its obvious creakiness, but I think it is actually quite wrong. Wilde invites this reading, to be sure, but he also wants us to see through
it. The problems with it are many. First, it is artistically quite un-
satisfactory and out of keeping with the general tenor of the
book. Why should there be this sudden inexplicable appeal to divine retribution backed up with supernatural infusions? Why

did God wait till that moment to finish Dorian off? Where was God during the rest of the story? Is stabbing someone in the heart the kind of thing we expect of God? And if we are to suppose that the devil did it, then why would he see fit to murder Dorian, instead of just letting him assume the appearance of the destroyed painting? The whole idea is artistically shabby, a piece of careless story-telling. But further, there are problems of mundane detail. How come the picture is undamaged if Dorian stuck a knife into it? Did he first slash it and then God (or the devil) stepped in to sew it seamlessly up again? Why would God do that? How precisely did the knife get into Dorian's heart if he plunged it into the picture? Did it just take to the air of its own accord, having slipped from Dorian's grasp, and aim itself into his chest? Or did God turn Dorian's hand against him, so that he watched his own hand do the stabbing against his will? Both ideas seem farfetched. Also, if you want to destroy a picture, so that no trace of it is left, you don't *stab* it, you burn it, as Dorian had arranged for Basil's body to be burned. The evidence of the hideous face would still be there after a mere stabbing. And isn't the word 'crash' not quite right for the sound of a human body falling to the floor? That is certainly the right word for a falling picture, but 'thud' would be more appropriate for the sound of Dorian's body hitting the floor. Why does Wilde use the word 'crash' if no picture fell? And if it did fall, only to be hoisted back up again, then why do we not hear a second sound as Dorian falls? Why does Wilde seem to suggest that the picture fell and then apparently go back on this suggestion? Cheap suspense? Poor writing?

But more telling than any of these technical questions, there is the problem of motivation and context. As I noted above, it is clear from the earlier incident with Hetty Merton that Dorian has reached the point at which he is absolutely incapable of performing a decent action, even when he tries to, and that he therefore has no way out of his moral predicament, except through suicide. Merely to remove the picture from his life will do nothing to improve the moral condition of his soul, yet despair over this is what prompts him to do the stabbing. Suicide is the inevitable way out: it is what we expect of him at this stage of the story. So the stabbing in the attic must be interpreted as an act of suicide. But how could he expect to commit suicide just by destroying the painting? He could hardly have foreseen the bizarre and miraculous occurrence that allegedly took place. The superficial reading cannot allow that his intentions were suicidal in this final scene, yet that is what the logic of the story requires. Dorian is by this stage a murderer of his closest friend, a blackmailer, a drug addict, an object of obloquy and hatred, the cause of several suicides, quite beyond moral redemption, nothing but a corrupt shell of a man: he is a pawn of the devil, his soul a hideous parody of his earlier beauty. His future promises only more of the same, as well as the constant threat of exposure. Death is the only solution for him; thus death is what he must have been aiming at when he took the knife into his hand. But the superficial reading cannot allow for this.

Let us then try out the reading I have been suggesting: that Dorian has *become* the picture. According to this suggestion, 'the canvas' and 'the picture' have come to have different referents, while earlier they denoted the same thing; in particular, 'the picture' now refers to Dorian the peripatetic art work. We must read Wilde as being sly and ironic and playful with his use of these words—traits not exactly out of character for that author. What the text says is subtle: seeing the knife he used to kill Basil, Dorian thinks: 'it had killed the painter, so it would kill the painter's work, and all that it meant.' But of course Dorian *is* 'the painter's work', as he is also Henry's work—they both created him as he is. What Dorian has become—a timeless beautiful monster of corruption—is precisely the work of the painter: *this* is what the painter wrought. This is why the verb 'kill' is the right word for what Dorian intends, as it would not be if he were merely out to destroy the canvas (one does not *kill* a canvas). The *canvas* is no longer the painter's work, because it has changed beyond recognition—Basil did not paint a hideous old man; only Dorian preserves the original image, and he does so because of the painter's idolatrous art (and his own pact). There is thus linguistic room for the suicidal intention. He also says that he will kill 'this monstrous soul-life', and that too would be accomplished by killing himself, since the soul that now resides in the vicinity of the canvas will die with him—it is *his*, after all.

Wilde next writes: 'He seized the thing, and stabbed the picture with it.' On my interpretation, this is to say that he stabbed *himself*, since he is the picture; *he never plunged the knife into the canvas at all*. Neither did he have any intention of doing so. This is precisely the reason that the canvas is found intact on the wall and why the knife is found in Dorian's heart. Its trajectory was never from canvas to person, because Dorian simply plunged it into his own chest in an act of straightforward suicide. As we are led to expect, he *must* commit suicide by this stage, and he does so in the obvious way—by stabbing himself in the heart. It is just that, since he is now the picture, to do this he needs to stab 'the picture'. There is no magical motion of the knife from the canvas into his heart, with the canvas then unripping itself; the knife never went near the canvas. The cry comes from Dorian and so does the crash. The word 'crash' is carefully chosen to effect the identification of Dorian with the picture; it has exactly the right ambiguity and suggestiveness. The picture *did* crash to the floor, just as we are at first led to believe, but that is because *Dorian* does, and he *is* the picture. So everything happens quite logically and naturally without the benefit of a *deus ex machina*. He stabs himself with the intention of committing suicide, and there follows a simple annulment of the previous pact, as his soul is extinguished. By forcing mortality on himself he abrogates the original contract, so he takes on the mortality that is properly his. He steps out of the sphere of art, reversing his earlier transition, and back into life. The picture itself then shifts its location again, while all the while remaining unchanged: *it* has never for a second been anything other than perfect and immortal. All that has happened is that the painter's art has manifested itself at different places: it now hangs on the wall again, where it belongs.

What Wilde has done is to condense the general theme of his book into this final scene, giving it literal expression, so that Dorian's odd ambiguous status, suspended between life and art, is represented. The pact gave him eternal beauty by converting him into a work of art; now he chooses to cancel his status as artwork. He never destroys the art-work, which is imperishable, but only takes his own mortal life. The original work still hangs magnificently on the wall, quite unchanged, while he is reduced to mere mortality—sin, age, death. The final scene, then, is entirely consonant with the interpretation I am suggesting, and in fact is baffling without that interpretation. Certainly, the book and its conclusion are a lot more satisfying under this interpretation than under the superficial reading.

Some very early passages in the book bear out this interpretation by preparing the ground for the identification of person and picture. Dorian complains to Basil, 'I am no more to you than a green bronze figure' (50), and indeed Basil has earlier described Dorian as 'simply a motive in art' (33). His attitude to Dorian is that of the artist to his subject—Dorian is primarily a source of aesthetic contemplation and inspiration. He exists to be gazed at and aesthetically appreciated. At a later point there is some discussion as to who is the 'real Dorian', the picture or the man, with Basil declaring, 'I shall stay with the real Dorian'(53), meaning the portrait—Dorian being about to accompany Henry to the theatre (itself a place where representations gather). Here already we have the suggestion that the status of representation has shifted from one location to another: for if the canvas contains the real Dorian, who is the Dorian strolling around London? At this early stage of the story, then, doubts are already being raised as to what is represented and what does the representing. Most tellingly and explicitly, we have the exchange in which Basil makes to destroy the painting himself after it has caused Dorian to lament the loss of youth he must endure. Dorian intervenes, saying: 'Don't, Basil, don't! . . . It would be murder' (51). That could be so only if the picture had ceased to be merely a picture. Then Dorian says of the picture: 'I am in love with it, Basil. It is part of myself. I feel that' (51). He is already merging with the picture, absorbing it into himself, or being absorbed by it. And in case we are still missing the point Basil replies: 'Well, as soon as you are dry, you shall be varnished, and framed, and sent home. Then you can do what you like with yourself' (51). The painting is him now, while he is left to be a mere depiction of it. Art has usurped life, converting life into art and itself into life. It has acquired a kind of ontological authority, even omnipotence. It exerts supernatural power over Dorian; in the end, demonic power. It engulfs him, making of him a mere puppet, a slave of art. Here Wilde is attributing to the artist a kind of magical gift: he can cast a spell over us, making us what we are not. In the case of Dorian, he is transformed by art *into* art, as these early passages indicate. Once the portrait exists his own identity becomes moot.

3. THE LIMITS OF AESTHETICISM

There is one cardinal point of our story that not even the most casual reader could miss: that the face of Dorian's soul, grinning and leering behind its purple cloth in the attic, is exceptionally, eye-peelingly, ugly. It is not a pleasure to gaze upon. It inspires nothing but disgust and loathing. It is, as it were, the precise aesthetic opposite of the beautiful face that caused its present decay. Not one particle of affection or admiration could it conceivably evoke.

But what is the significance of this fact for the overall thrust of the novel? What lesson does it teach? Clearly matters have come to a sorry head: none of this ought to have happened. Basil's painting, abetted by Lord Henry's panegyric to youth and beauty, has issued in this extreme ugliness, with all that it morally represents. The tale is manifestly a tragic one. The moral order has been disturbed, and the results are catastrophic for all concerned. The happiness that Henry predicted for Dorian has come to nothing but grief and death. In no sense has Henry's philosophy been corroborated. The story is thus a morally conservative one in its upshot. It tells of the moral dangers of art and the aesthetic impulse. Clearly Dorian should not have made the pact he did: he should have accepted that he is not a work of art, timelessly beautiful and immutable; he should have acknowledged the realities of age and mortality.

Likewise, Basil's idolatrous infatuation with Dorian's beauty has brought about both his own notably gruesome death (overseen by his own distorted handiwork) and the ruin and death of many others. He, along with Henry, caused Dorian to try to live his life guided only by aesthetic standards, finding beauty even in depravity and death. Extracting aesthetic pleasure from Sybil's suicide is plainly morally despicable and is intended by Wilde to be found so. The extreme ugliness of Dorian's soul is the measure of the error of his ways, and it is a measure that even the most ardent aesthete can understand. Even Dorian's mentor, Lord Henry, is depicted as a bit of a sad case by the novel's end—a man so afraid of death and suffering that he fabricates far-fetched philosophical theories in order to avoid facing reality. His marriage is in ruins (it was always a hollow and shabby pretence).

His two closest friends are violently killed. He speaks darkly of inner sorrows.

The aesthetic impulse is thus shown to be top-heavy, perilously primed, in the case of all three of the main characters. They are dazzled and blinded by beauty, worshipping it beyond its due. Art attracts them with a bright alluring flame, but they all end up burned by it. Henry's relatively unscathed end is doubtless owed to the boasted insincerity with which he propounds his theories of aesthetics and morality. Dorian took Henry's all-out aestheticism seriously, and he ended up with a soul that no aesthete could countenance. The ugliness of his portrait is simply a mark of the evil that has come to permeate the story. It issues its verdict over what has come before.

This brings us to the nerve of the book, and what I take to be its most brilliant contrivance. For there is a glaring irony in Dorian's story: by pursuing beauty alone, spurning all moral restraint, he ends up making the very core of his being as hideous as anything could be. The outward beauty of his life is purchased at the cost of extreme inner ugliness. By making sin into art he makes his soul into a gargoyle—the very antithesis of the beautiful. That is to say: his aesthetic project is actually *self-refuting* or *self-undermining*. He wants to be nothing but beautiful, treating even evil as an occasion for aesthetic exploitation, but the result is ugliness in his very soul. To deny the claims of morality, in the service of an aesthetic ideal, is precisely to make one's soul hideous; so to reject morality in the name of love of beauty is to negate one's aim. The reason for this is simply that an evil character is an ugly character. It is because the aesthetic theory of virtue is true, as I have explained that theory in the previous chapter, that Dorian has undertaken an impossible project. Beauty cannot be *opposed* to virtue, because virtue itself involves a form of beauty. This is the fundamental fallacy in the aestheticism propounded by Lord Henry: he has forgotten that the aesthetic extends beyond the world of the senses. He has neglected *moral* beauty. Dorian's repulsive portrait is the concrete proof of that. When Henry responds to Dorian's plea that his soul not be hideous by saying that this is 'a very charming artistic basis for ethics' (126), he is in effect acknowledging the contradiction in his own philosophy. How can we reject morality in the name of beauty if that very rejection necessarily involves the creation of a singularly hideous object? Wilde's story takes the aesthetic theory of virtue as given—it is what the portrait embodies—and this is what refutes the kind of amoral aestheticism that Henry preaches and Dorian lives by. It is, if you like, a necessary conceptual truth that evil acts cannot be rendered beautiful, since they carry with them their own form of ugliness. The evil agent has an ugly soul, so it is not possible to beautify the evil life through and through. (Perhaps this is why Henry also preaches shallowness as wisdom: it is the only way he can avoid the contradiction in his own philosophy.)

It is important to appreciate that the paradox of aestheticism arises only when art attempts to usurp or smother ethics—when it tries to find beauty in evil and to pursue evil for the sake of the beauty to be invested in it. At a highly significant moment in the book, after describing Dorian's fascination with elaborate royal murders, along with embroidery and priestly vestments, Wilde writes: 'There were moments when he looked on evil as simply a mode through which he could realize his conception of the beautiful' (179). Yet, of course, in so doing he makes his soul ever more hideous. Here then is the paradox, as plain as a pikestaff: and it sets a logical limit to aestheticism. If we employ evil to express or contrive beauty, by being (say) an exquisitely refined torturer, an artist of rack and thumbscrew, then we inevitably generate ugliness somewhere in ourselves. Morality must win against aestheticism *even on aestheticism's own terms*. The only possible form of comprehensive aestheticism is one that *includes* morality. An aestheticism that opposes morality is necessarily unstable. The true aesthete must be a moralist, since he cares about the beauty of his soul. In a way, the fault in Lord Henry's philosophy, as enacted by Dorian, is that it is not aesthetic enough. The two men have misconceived the proper form of an aesthetic approach to life. That is the real upshot of Wilde's story. The ugly portrait is in itself a palpable reminder that beauty cannot be detached from virtue. Dorian and Henry in effect oppose one *kind* of beauty to another, sensuous versus moral, not beauty *tout court* against morality. And the result is that moral beauty emerges as the more powerful. We might well read the entire story as a plea for moral beauty—at least in its underlying structure. It comes out solidly in favour of moral aestheticism, not the amoral kind practised by Henry and Dorian.

This is not the outlook commonly associated with Oscar Wilde: we think of him as sharing Lord Henry's philosophy of morally cynical aestheticism (they certainly sound very much alike). Did not Wilde scorn traditional virtue in favour of dandyism, sensation-seeking, freedom of spirit? The aphorisms that preface the novel *sound* as if they are endorsing such a morally cleansed outlook. But his story points to a very different conclusion. What Wilde has done is to map the inherent limits of the aesthete's viewpoint. He has taken aestheticism seriously and asked whether aesthetic value might be the only sort of value worth pursuing, even to the point of trying to render evil aesthetically appealing. His conclusion, as represented in the story, is twofold. First, this leads to destruction, despair, and sorrow for all concerned. Second, the amoral aesthete's position is simply not fully consistent, given that the realm of the aesthetic must incorporate the moral: it is not *possible* to pursue beauty in all its forms without pursuing virtue. At his death, Dorian even becomes *physically* hideous, as his inner being rises to the surface, so that he has not finally protected himself from the kind of sensuous ugliness he has striven to avoid. And he is far uglier now than he ever would have been had he lived his life without the pact. His amoral devotion to his own physical beauty has finally resulted in a truly hideous physical appearance. We can only imagine what Lord Henry would think when presented with this wrinkled and deformed paradigm of the anti-aesthetic—his beautiful friend transformed into a hideous monster. Not merely ugliness of soul has resulted from his aestheticism; even ugliness of body has been the final upshot.

No doubt there are genuine attractions in Lord Henry's philosophy, felt by Wilde as much as the reader: beauty *is* good, traditional morality *is* often irrational and hypocritical, art *can* act as a palliative for the pain of life (and death). It is therefore tempting to try to make art and beauty into the sole realities. But the aesthetic impulse must nevertheless be curbed; it cannot be granted unrestricted scope. Or rather: it must be morally informed or else it will lead to an ugliness that lies too close to home. Put simply, beauty and evil cannot coexist. This is, we might say, a *theorem* of the aesthetic theory of virtue—as well as being a piece of plain common sense. The fate of Dorian Gray exemplifies this truth: his evil drives out his beauty, first internally, and then even externally. His fate is to become hideous from every viewpoint. The irony here could hardly be heavier.

4. THE RELEVANCE OF *DORIAN GRAY*

I have examined this story not only because of its conceptual interest but also because I believe that Wilde is treating a subject of great relevance to human life. We are, among other things, aesthetically sensitive beings, capable of viewing ourselves and others as aesthetic objects, and this carries its moral perils. It is easy and natural for us to see ourselves as players in a drama, each endowed with our own quantum of aesthetic value. We impose art on events. Thus real tragedies can strike us, as they struck Dorian, as merely moments in a drama; and there is entertainment value in such moments (television is jammed with this kind of thing). We are also prone to value each other in proportion to our aesthetic appeal, in ways that scarcely need to be specified.[3] The aesthetic tendency can therefore conflict with other moral values; the two sets of values do not exist in perfect harmony. And it is simply wrong to let the aesthetic dominate over the moral. Life should *not* be made into art in this way. Suffering and death are what they are, prosaically and horribly, and no amount of aesthetics can change their nature. Trying to conceal their nature under the mantle of art, tempting though it may be, can only lead to self-deception and catastrophe. We need to oppose this kind of aestheticism, not to encourage it. In the first instance, we need to be *aware* of it.

Wilde's story in fact endorses the simple virtues of kindness, consideration, honesty, loyalty, modesty, restraint, acceptance of life. It sees that these lack the glitter of the (sensuously) aesthetic, but it insists on them anyway. What is interesting is that it reaches this common-sense conclusion on the basis of an elaborate and sophisticated exploration of the relationship between morality and beauty. It uses art to show that art is not all there is to care about. Or better: it argues for a form of beauty that might

[3] There is a bitingly funny passage in Kingsley Amis's *Lucky Jim* in which the advantages enjoyed by the good-looking are fearlessly tabulated: 242–3. Speaking of Christine's superiority in looks over Margaret, the narrator reflects that 'there was no end of ways in which nice things are nicer than nasty things'.

seem removed from art in the conventional sense. This means that there is a way to reconcile the aesthetic and the moral—by acknowledging that the two are ultimately inseparable, as argued in the previous chapter. The achievement of *Dorian Gray* is to raise this question in a dramatically shapely form and to indicate how it is best resolved. The concept of the beautiful soul emerges as the only way to keep the aesthetic impulse under proper control.

A final word about deception. At one point, soon after murdering Basil, Dorian 'for a moment felt keenly the terrible pleasure of a double life' (210). He enjoyed, that is, the systematic deception that his life had come to require—the thrill experienced by the smooth and expert liar. But in his case the doubling has a special meaning: in one life he is beautiful, graceful, and charming; in another he is grotesque, violent, and repulsive. He runs on divergent aesthetic rails, and it is necessary that this fact should be kept from the world. He survives by systematic aesthetic deception. In this respect he dramatizes the common human condition: we must all live a dual aesthetic life to some degree, and the possibility (or necessity) of deception is always present.[4] Aesthetic deception is a fact of human life, potentially or actually. Dorian simply takes it to new heights.

This brings action and the will into the picture. Dorian has two modes of concealment of his inner ugliness: his naturally given looks, and his modes of behaviour. His good looks have been supernaturally guaranteed, so that they will not give his inner secret away; but his actions are under his control, and they may well disclose what his looks conceal. He is still capable of the ugly gesture, the ghastly expression, the jarring utterance. Thus he must practise willed deception—though this is made easier for him by the illusion of virtue his face and figure present. Here is the juncture at which his inner ugliness is liable to show itself, despite the flawless beauty of the bodily vehicle. Action works as a kind of bridge between the two aesthetic levels, since it has a foot both in the mind of the person and in his bodily appearance.

---

[4] This duality often strikes me most strongly at the gym, because one has to parade speechlessly in a semi-clothed state, thus revealing one's physical form while keeping one's soul to oneself. The emphasis on the body accentuates its aesthetic distinctness from the mind. Perhaps models and the like feel this schism all the time.

Willed deception is necessary because of this fact about action; Dorian cannot simply relax and let his face take care of the problem of deceiving others. Action is a third locale at which personal beauty, or the lack of it, can manifest itself. The flawless face can on occasion be contorted by a loathsome expression—the sneer of cruelty, the hard stare of hatred, the pinched mouth of meanness. Here the ugly soul erupts into the beautiful body, as it were, causing a strangely disconcerting aesthetic dissonance in the beholder. Hence the necessity of constant deception on the part of the internally flawed. The stock character of the exquisitely mannered sadist is a case in point: she needs to cloak her inner vileness in an exaggerated show of grace. Thus a certain human type is born: those who live by the carefully calibrated gesture, designed for maximum aesthetic effect, but whose inner landscape is bleak and repellent. Such individuals are particularly dangerous, since they can project an impression of virtue that they signally lack. It is all too easy to be taken in by them.

Deception of this kind is therefore naturally viewed as especially morally odious. To conceal one's inner nature in this way invites misplaced trust, an assumption of virtue. Dorian Gray's portrait surely owes much of its foulness to the sin of deception that its subject systematically perpetrates on those around him. For this sin is the precondition of the possibility of his other sins. But the cost is a boiling inner ugliness that finally bursts to the surface and carves itself into his face. He personifies moral and aesthetic mendacity, taking it to extremes that no ordinary mortal could hope to match. Those among us who operate by lesser versions of the same strategy are welcome to take him as their model and hero. It would no doubt be too much to hope that they will suffer a similar fate.

7

Who is Frankenstein's Monster?

1. THE MEANING OF MONSTROSITY

The monster has always been with us. Misshapen, deformed, hideous, terrifying—the monster prowls and lurks, bent on doing us unprecedented damage. He is strong, agile, determined. His nature is to be preternatural, yet he is generally mortal, not quite purely demonic. He uses no weapons, save those native to him. His place is the forest, the cave, the woodshed, the laboratory, the remote galaxy, the sky, the sea. He belongs where we fear to tread, in alien elements. But he is curiously fixated on us; he will not leave us alone. He needs us. We, in turn, dread him— yet he can sometimes excite our sympathy. We are troubled and excited by his existence. The monster is a rich source of human anxiety. He is always with us because we invite him to stay close. [The many monsters of myth, folklore, and fiction no doubt represent some deep psychological truth about us. We are their creators, the source of their monstrosity; they have the attributes we give to them. We are both their authors and their victims.] We bring them on ourselves. We cause them to exist and then they come back to haunt us. The human imagination is thus given to monstrosity; from its fertile soil spring fiends of every kind.

What do these monsters mean? I would suggest, in line with the previous two chapters, that they act as visible embodiments of evil, by way of the idea that evil is a form of ugliness. If the evil spirit were to become visible, *this* is how it would look—as 'ugly as sin'. We take the notion of evil as ugliness of soul and concretize it in the form of a monster of physically repellent aspect. We take evil out of its hiding place in the soul and display it for all to see. The monster is evil writ palpable, and hence more easily grasped and detected. Monsters exist, in effect, because of the psychic entrenchment of the aesthetic theory of virtue. They are a reification of the soul made ugly through vice and innate depravity.

Some exceptional humans achieve the status of monster by their own actions, and when they do their physical appearance is apt to assume the aspect of the grotesque. Their evil seems to concentrate itself in their features, as the face becomes a repellent mask. Consider the face of Adolf Hitler, to take the stock example: it personifies ruthless, crazed destructiveness and cruelty, as if hardly able to contain the evil raging below the surface—a face tight and creased with mad violence. That little liquorice moustache—in itself a silly stripe aboard an insecure upper lip—comes to seem the very mark of organized viciousness, a sort of death signature. A thin one-inch strip of facial hair has become fearful and repellent (who now will venture such a moustache?). The ascription of evil thus makes us attribute monstrous features to the evil individual. In this way we identify the domestic monsters amongst us—those who outstrip their fellows in the extent and quality of their evil. The connection between evil and outer monstrosity is deeply entrenched in our thought and imagination.

But this simple picture becomes immediately complicated once a particular monster is considered in its entirety. For the monster must not merely be a physical expression of *our* inner life, but must also have an inner life of its own. And what is this to be like, aesthetically speaking? What will be its state of virtue? It *tends* also to be monstrous, given the reason for which the monster is originally contrived. But there is no logical necessity about that: the monster *might* not have an ugly interior. He, like us, runs on separate aesthetic rails, and hence need not duplicate within himself his outer hideousness. Thus there is room for an imaginative creation that both expresses spiritual evil in its appearance but also harbours an innocent virtuous nature of its own. This being will be the aesthetic converse of Dorian Gray, whose outer beauty belies his inner corruption. Such a combination will inevitably provoke ambivalent feelings in us: there we have the outer symbol of evil, exemplified in the body, but it has become detached from its usual spiritual referent. Good and evil are joined in the same individual, throwing us off our moral balance. Should we flee from this individual or embrace him (despite his repulsiveness)? But the combination will also produce an object of considerable fascination for us—an entity that tests our moral and aesthetic categories, forcing us to think harder about how we employ them. The inwardly attractive monster occupies its own anomalous and unique position in logical space. It is a challenge to our assumptions as well as to our ordinary human reactions. It is the monster-concept come of age.

Just such a being is the creature created by Mary Shelley in *Frankenstein*,[1] written around 1816 when the author was a mere nineteen years old, scarcely out of adolescence. In this book Victor Frankenstein, a driven and brilliant scientist, himself creates a monster for reasons of scientific advancement and human amelioration. Shelley creates the monster for us to contemplate imaginatively, while Frankenstein has more practical motives. We and he both feel a complex of emotions about this creature (hereafter 'the Creature': he is never given the dignity of a name). He tests our sympathies and understanding, as we go from feeling compassion for his plight to reviling him for his violent response to it. It is not easy to analyse these feelings and reactions, to come to a just assessment of the case. This is no doubt part of the fascination of the novel. I think it is true to say, in a general way, that the Creature provokes both love and loathing in us, esteem and condemnation, trust and fear; we are simultaneously attracted to him and repelled by him. His internal aesthetic configuration shifts and mutates, and in intelligible ways, despite the constancy of his physical appearance. There is a continuous interplay between his interior and his exterior, mediated by human responses to him. The chief architects of his spiritual shape are the hostile humans he encounters. He is originally a kind of blank tablet upon which the actions of others are imprinted. His story is complex, pregnant, and salutary—an emblematic tale of moral metamorphosis.

There is much that can be said about this monster and his scientific creator, but I want to focus on a particular question about the story, namely: why are we so fascinated by it? This story has exercised a powerful and sustained appeal since its initial publication in 1818. It has entered and permeated modern culture, es-

---

[1] Page references in the text are to the edition cited in the Bibliography. I shall assume some familiarity with the story. I might mention that the book is much richer and more interesting than the film versions might suggest.

pecially popular culture. Everyone has heard of Frankenstein (even if many think this to be the name of the monster, not of its human progenitor). Even those who have not read the book but have seen the many films based upon it, loosely or otherwise, or have just heard the basic story, are gripped by it. It seems to strike some deep chord in us. And this cannot be merely because it exemplifies the general notion of the monster as moral emblem, since the appeal seems specific and unique. Something about *this* monster evokes our intense interest and concern.

What is it about him that makes him so transfixing to us? To be sure, this is a good story, well told, with much drama and thrilling horror. And the theme of the dangers of unbridled science is apposite and has only grown in importance since the book was written. But concern over the dangers of nuclear weapons, genetic engineering, intelligent robots, bacteriological research, and so forth cannot be what lies behind the peculiar resonance the story has. Our focus on the Creature himself is far too specific for that. If the appeal of the vampire stories is at least partly sexual, thus accounting for their special fascination, then what does the appeal of the story of the man-made monster, stitched together from dead body parts and roaming the land, depend upon? What do we find in this creature's specific nature that so engages us? I do not mean to be asking what Mary Shelley *intended* to achieve in creating her monster; I mean to ask why in *fact*, whatever her conscious (or unconscious) intentions might have been, do *we* respond to the story with the fascination we do. What does he *mean* to us?

A natural answer is that he represents the dangerous alien other. He is the abnormal inhuman threat, the brutal invader from beyond, the lost member of some remote and terrible tribe. He belongs to some strange and predatory species, parodying our own. He comes into our midst, in all his oddity and otherness, to visit upon us his barbarous and opaque desires. He is the threatening unknown, the creature from the Other Side. He belongs with those invaders from space or devils from hell or species cross-breeds of myth. Or, perhaps, he represents those few unfortunate humans marginalized because of their physical divergence from the norm—the hunchbacked or birthmarked or burned or otherwise deformed. In any case, his essence is otherness: he is not 'one of us'. His physical ugliness marks him off from the run of humanity. This is the obvious way to read the story. Victor Frankenstein is depicted, at least to begin with, as a normal, healthy, attractive, successful young man, with an exceptionally loving family and a devoted cousin who is soon to become his wife. Victor's father is a paternal paragon—kind, reasonable, trustworthy. So, too, Captain Walton, who begins the narrative by finding Victor half-dead in the Antarctic, is a normal happy man with a mission and a devoted sister. The alien disruptive element in all this calm and sanity is the monster Victor creates in an excess of scientific zeal, though with the highest humanitarian intentions. The Creature is superhumanly strong and agile, resilient, gigantic, fearsomely ugly, and delivered into the world in a highly unorthodox fashion. His birth and upbringing are anything but normal. What could be more different from us than a being assembled from parts of dead bodies and brought to life artificially? He has no family, no friends, no mate, no childhood to speak of, no home, no name. He is alone in the world and desperate. He envies his creator his ideal family, while resenting his own exclusion from human society, resolving in the end to destroy the happiness of the man who gave him life—his 'father'. This is surely (it is natural to think) the exceptional story of a radical outsider, one whose contrast with the normal human lot could hardly be greater.

His first seriously violent act, after suffering the unjust rejection and hostility of the people he encounters, is to strangle Victor's young brother, William. He describes the moment thus: 'I gazed on my victim, and my heart swelled with exultation and hellish triumph; clapping my hands, I exclaimed, "I too can create desolation; my enemy is not invulnerable; this death will carry despair to him, and a thousand other miseries shall torment and destroy him"' (138). This murder of an innocent child is manifestly an exceptional act, and the Creature's jubilant response is exceptional too. It is evil on a grand and abnormal scale. This is the kind of thing we fear from the barbaric other—the evil that knows no human restraint or remorse. It is truly monstrous. Thus what we find in the Creature is a focus for our fear of the ferocious unruly other. Supernatural, yet existing on the fringes of humanity, he stands for everything counter to our normal life—a creature cut from alien cloth. We might compare him to the predatory beast of the aptly named film *Alien*.[2] This creature from outer space, as inexorable and resourceful as it is repulsive, comes into a normal human environment from an unexplored planet, and proceeds to wreak murderous havoc. Its mode of reproduction is quite unlike our own, reaching viability by bursting through the stomach of the unlucky individual who has been made host to its earlier larva-like stages. It *looks* quite inhuman, a combination of insect, robot, and reptile. The fascination of this creature lies in its contrast to us—the sense we have of a being operating according to different rules. In the same way, it might naturally be thought, Frankenstein's monster intrudes from an alien element into human society, there to terrorize and destroy. That is his narrative function, his dramatic significance. His mercilessness and jubilation at killing a child are an indication of his essential inhumanity.

So it would be natural to suppose, and certainly there are many other fictional monsters that have stood for our fear of the alien, well-grounded or not. But I think that in this case such an interpretation misses the mark completely: Frankenstein's monster is *us*; we see *ourselves* in him; in him we see our *own* nature. His story is our story, writ gigantic and ugly. His is the normal human condition—not literally, of course, but metaphorically, symbolically. It is because of our tacit identification with this monster that he fascinates us in the way he does. We read into his life aspects of our own existence, aspects we prefer to ignore. Let me then retell his story, in roughly chronological order, with this interpretation in mind. Prepare to hear the truth about yourself.

+ p. 168

2. THE HUMAN MONSTER

The story is constructed as a sequence of three narratives, each nested in the one before: first Captain Walton's, who takes Victor onto his ship in bleakest Antarctica; second Victor's, as he reports to Walton how he came to his present sorry condition; third the Creature's, detailing his life story and wishes to Victor. Then the sequence of narrators is reversed, with Walton finishing the story.

---

[2] *Alien*, directed by Ridley Scott, 1979.

Each segment is told in the first person, and each represents a distinct perspective on what has happened. The Creature is glimpsed at the very beginning by Walton, racing in a sled across the icy wastes, and at the end, hovering over the deathbed of his creator. Victor tells us of the Creature's origins and of his dealings with him as one catastrophe follows another. It is left to the Creature himself to bring his nature into focus for us, by reporting his experiences at first hand. This structure permits the true character of the Creature to be gradually unfolded, so that there is a shock of recognition when we begin to enter into his most intimate thoughts and emotions. Early suggestions of affinity between him and us culminate in a torrent of intelligible human experience. The Creature moves closer to our own condition as we approach nearer to his life. We take a journey into his interior and find there a familiar face.

But first we must go back to the Creature's physical origins— the means by which he comes into the world. No act of human sexual intercourse inaugurates his existence; instead, he is composed of dead tissues taken from the corpses that Victor has gathered and dismantled, and then assembled into a full humanlike figure. By means of a scientific discovery Victor is loath to disclose to us, this composite body has the spark of life infused into it. Once the parts are properly combined and the requisite life-giving pulse is pumped into the body, it jolts and twitches into sentience. No womb cushions its transition from mere insensate matter into a conscious subject thrown into the world. The moment of the Creature's birth is described thus by Victor:

It was on a dreary night of November, that I beheld the accomplishment of my toils. With an anxiety that amounted almost to agony, I collected the instruments of life around me, that I might infuse a spark of being into the lifeless thing that lay at my feet. It was already one in the morning; the rain pattered dismally against the panes, and my candle was nearly burnt out, when, by the glimmer of the half-extinguished light, I saw the dull yellow eye of the creature open; it breathed hard, and a convulsive motion agitated its limbs. (56)

Life and feeling blink abruptly into being, on a rainy night in a dismal room: there is now a new centre of consciousness in existence, about to be confronted by reality. That reality includes the manner of its own creation and its physical composition.

It is not difficult to interpret these beginnings as an allegory of our own creation. For it is equally true that the tissues that compose *us* originate from insentient matter of various unsavoury sorts, which are united to form a living conscious being. There is the sperm and ovum from which you grow—those improbable blobs of senseless organic material—and there is the food your mother consumes that gets converted into bone, muscle, brain tissue, and all the rest. Somehow this congeries of disparate materials becomes a conscious being as the foetus develops, by mechanisms not yet fully understood. Electrical activity in the nervous system appears crucial to the onset of consciousness and to motor activity—as it was crucial to the Creature's creation as a conscious being. It is really a stunning truth, one that we need to be reminded of—though we are always tacitly aware of it—that we are all collections of material particles brought together from diverse and unpromising sources into a hunk of bloody meat. Our bodies are admittedly stitched together by natural threads, but they are still contingent clumps of once-dead stuff. The tissues that compose us have constituents that were once parts of cabbages and pigs and excrement and worms and fragments of other planets and the soup of energy that followed the Big Bang. (It would be amusing to write a story about the career of a single particle as it takes up residence over the aeons in the bodies of different objects and organisms: our pet particle might boast to its particle colleagues of the distinguished sites it has fleetingly occupied.) Indeed, just as the Creature is composed of other people's bodies, so we are probably partly composed of matter that was once part of other people's bodies: the worms eat the corpses, the birds eat the worms, we eat the birds. And of course the body of the foetus is wholly composed of matter from the mother's body, specifically her blood. We all have our origin in coagulated bits of dead matter drawn from accidental sources, and not delightful to dwell upon. From one perspective, all life is just the contingent redistribution of inanimate materials—a kind of momentary swirl in the void.

We are also assemblages of organs upon whose proper functioning our lives depend. Most of these organs lie hidden beneath the skin, and are not generally regarded as lovely to behold. The operating table reveals all those wet tubes and pulsing vessels, to our discomfort and repulsion. Even the most beautiful body is a grisly sight inside—down among the internal organs. The kidneys or colon of the supermodel are no more attractive than yours or mine. Frankly, our bodies are pretty repulsive once you dig below the surface. Our own aesthetic sense turns from their full reality. It is notable that in one of the very few descriptions of the Creature's physical appearance we are directed to consider his subdermal workings: 'His limbs were in proportion, and I had selected his features as beautiful. Beautiful!—Great God! His yellow skin scarcely covered the work of muscles and arteries beneath . . .' (56). This reminds us of what *our* skin so thinly and fragilely conceals, and hence of what our bodies really are. To say 'animal' misses the mark; 'monstrous' is far more to the point. And, just as the assembly of these subdermal parts was gruesome and bloody in the case of the Creature, so too must the normal process be, to human aesthetic sensibility, when seen up close. Who, save the professionally inured, does not feel a queasy twinge when contemplating the organic construction of the foetus? Doctors, notoriously, must dull their natural aesthetic sense, or develop a new one ('The human renal system is really, to us doctors, a *beautiful* natural object, though it may not seem so to the layman . . .'). Thus we are all Frankensteinian monsters under the skin. He is not supposed to be uglier *there* than we are. Our beauty is, quite literally, skin deep (and if you start looking at the skin under a microscope you will be in for some severe aesthetic shocks). In the Creature we see traces of the assembly process, and of what is assembled, in the scars and stitching, so that we are made aware of the full bodily reality of his being; but we too are in fundamentally the same case—with the joins less visible, the insides more hidden.

The Creature feels bodily shame; he is aware of his deformity and keenly laments it.

I had admired the perfect forms of my cottagers—their grace, beauty, and delicate complexions: but how was I terrified, when I viewed myself in a transparent pool! At first I started back, unable to believe that it was indeed I who was reflected in the mirror; and when I became fully convinced that I was in reality the monster I am, I was filled with the bitterest sensations of despondence and mortification. (110)

But such bodily shame is not unknown to us, especially in circumstances that remove our normal aesthetic protection. I have already mentioned the surgery table and the doctor's office, but there is also the matter of sexual intimacy, during which the body's secrets are apt to be abruptly revealed. The sexual organs themselves, though plainly erotic, are not generally deemed *beautiful*. The question of the Creature's sexuality is indeed not shirked in the book, and the character of his reproductive organs is a subject not always distant from the surface. He does, in point of fact, request the creation of a female mate, with whom he may reproduce his kind. Monstrous congress is clearly contemplated. This serves to remind the reader of his or her own sexual body: if intercourse between the Creature and his would-be bride strikes us as aesthetically unappealing, might we not acknowledge a comparable uneasiness about our own bodies in this regard? Is the Creature's penis any *worse*, aesthetically, than the next man's? Bodily shame on behalf of the squelchy machine that composes us is common enough; the Creature is by no means the only embodied being to suffer from it. And, remembering the attitudes towards sexuality prevalent in England at the beginning of the nineteenth century, it is perhaps not surprising if Mary Shelley should exhibit some heightened responsiveness to the underlying issues of bodily shame. In sexual relations some of the true aesthetic nature of the body is made distressingly transparent.

None of what I have said is restricted to human beings who are physically abnormal in some way. In a certain sense, we are all malformed, all aesthetic catastrophes. We tend to protect ourselves from this thought, but the Creature reminds us of its inescapable truth—though in a displaced form that makes it easier to handle. The beauty of the human form is a sort of visual illusion in which the skin plays the role of the arrows in the Müller-Lyer illusion.[3] Even Dorian Gray was not beautiful under the skin (not to mention his spiritual deformity). In the Creature this illusion is done away with, so that the true nature of the body is revealed. In addition to this universality, however, there is also the matter of individual bodily anxiety—those specific physical characteristics we deem to reduce our aesthetic appeal. This subject is too familiar to require much comment beyond acknowledging its existence. The anxiety in question typically begins in

[3] This is the illusion in which two lines of equal length look unequal because of the difference in the angles of the arrow-heads at the ends of each line.

early adolescence, causing much pubescent distress. Everyone feels themselves to be physically imperfect, even to be seriously deformed in some way—the shape of the nose, the cut of the calf, the proximity of the eyes, the size of the ears, and so forth and so on. Not to mention pimples, teeth defects, unruly hair, etc. All this will have been close to the experience of Mary Shelley herself, a late adolescent at the time the book was composed. The sensibility of the Creature is indeed much like that of the hypersensitive adolescent at a number of points. I once read of a man who in adolescence was convinced that the back of his head stuck out to an abnormal degree and felt doomed by this supposed fact; actually his head was remarkably flat at the back, but that made little difference to the way he saw it. Such familiar human anxieties are all too similar to the distress the Creature suffers when he first sees himself in a mirror. Imagine reaching adulthood yourself never having seen your own reflection: what aesthetic shocks might lie in wait for you! The Creature is scarcely the first to feel despondence at his physical appearance, and to feel fated by it.

3. ISOLATION: FAMILY, FRIENDS, AND OTHERS

The family life of Victor Frankenstein is remarkably idealized in the story: it affords unqualified domestic felicity, unfailing kindness and concern, everything one could hope a loving family to offer. Victor's father, in particular, is a paternal paragon. Great stress is laid on the happiness to be found in the Frankenstein household; Victor is even joyfully betrothed to his perfect cousin, Elizabeth, with whom he was brought up as brother to sister. The family is treated as a source of pure and simple good feeling—the *summum bonum*. By contrast, the Creature is condemned to live entirely without family, an absolute orphan. He is barred from experiencing any of the familial bliss that Victor takes for granted. No sooner, indeed, is the Creature thrown into the world than he is abandoned by his creator, whom he regards, rightly enough, as his father. As he blinks into consciousness, Victor runs immediately from him, alarmed and repelled by what he has created.

How can I describe my emotions at this catastrophe, or how delineate the wretch whom with such infinite pains and care I had endeavoured to form? . . . I had worked hard for nearly two years, for the sole purpose of infusing life into an inanimate body . . . but now that I had finished, the beauty of the dream vanished, and breathless horror and disgust filled my heart. Unable to endure the aspect of the being I had created, I rushed out of the room, and continued a long time traversing my bedchamber, unable to compose my mind to sleep. (56)

The Creature is thus deserted by his 'father' at the very moment he comes into being; he never has a mother of any sort;[4] he is utterly without family ties.

It might then seem that the contrast between Victor and his creation, with respect to family links, could hardly be greater, and hence that the distance between ourselves and the Creature is correspondingly wide. But let us examine the matter through a less roseate lens. Isn't the Creature's predicament obliquely redolent of our own? Isn't there a kind of symbolic truth to his isolation and abandonment? He comes into the world at the will of another, having no say in the matter, and then is left to his own devices by a creator who cannot accept his paternal responsibilities. Victor wants to be rid of what he has created, now that he sees the fruit of his efforts. The Creature must survive as best he can by whatever natural resources he possesses. He has been cast adrift in a hostile universe. Now it is easy to translate this into the normal situation. None of us asks to be born: we are all catapulted into the world at the will of others and are expected to live on the world's terms. The umbilical cord is cut early and abruptly, and then we are essentially on our own. We must breathe and eat and move, all by ourselves. We are *separate beings*, self-contained systems. And we know this to be our essential nature—to be separate and distinct from others. The feeling of existential isolation, on-your-ownness, is a common human experience, derived from our basic metaphysical autonomy. The self is an enclosed and discontinuous entity, not part of some larger embracing psychic reality. We are created by others, but we do not *merge* with them; our identity is not theirs. We might say, 'I

---

[4] We hardly need the findings of modern clinical psychology to predict the psychological repercussions of this radical motherlessness. The Creature suffers from 'maternal deprivation' from the very beginning of his life and continuously thereafter. He is wholly without female influence.

exist, therefore I am separate.'[5] At birth we become physically separated from the mother's body, but we also, and more deeply, assume our role as an independent centre of consciousness. Our path through the world is ours alone; our experiences must be borne only by us. Birth—coming to exist—is inherently a flight between parent and child, a sudden pulling apart. For it necessarily involves the creation of an independent subject of consciousness. Thereafter, the family can only work to mitigate the fissure that is written ontologically into the structure of things. The ideal of continuity with others (overlap, immersion) is abrogated from the start.

A work of art or a piece of technology does not experience its distinctness from its creator, simply because it is not a conscious being; but we cannot avoid recognition of this; and a certain resentment attaches to it. The inevitable pain and strife of life are ours alone to bear, but we have been produced by others—without our assent—who do not have to bear our problems as we do. Isn't there something unfair about this? Where is the contract we signed to enter into such an arrangement? Our parents are the authors of our suffering, quite fundamentally, as of our essential aloneness. Thus, at a deep level, even the most responsible of parents will be felt to be falling down in what we require of them; for what we require *cannot* be satisfied, in the nature of the case. It is as if our consciousness is haunted by a metaphysical impossibility whose reality we nevertheless crave—the elimination of interpersonal boundaries. We dream, futilely, of a fusion of egos. And, of course, there are many areas where in fact parental responsibility is not exercised in the way it should be. In any case, the *feeling* of neglect must always be there, since the world does not always oblige the child's every whim. That is to say: we have an ideal of parental responsibility in which all our problems, even the pain of existence, even the fact of selfhood, will be shouldered by our parents. But this ideal is incapable of realization. Hence our brooding sense of resentment and abandonment. What Victor does to his creation is therefore just a dramatic version of what we all experience. He creates, and then he flees; just

[5] Descartes's *Cogito, ergo sum* (I think, therefore I am) shows (of course) only that *I* exist; no such argument can be used by me to show that *you* exist. This fundamental asymmetry demonstrates the irreducible plurality of selves—the essential otherness of the other. Hence the eternal threat of philosophical solipsism.

as, in making us, our parents make us *apart* from them. The parental bond is broken by its very creation, most basically by the mere fact of interpersonal distinctness. Parental 'desertion' is the common, and necessary, lot.

In addition to this, there is the undeniable burden that children bring. Victor wanted passionately to create a conscious living being, but as soon as it lives and breathes before him he is struck with the burden he has incurred. That can hardly be an uncommon experience, disturbing though it may be to admit it. How many people have rushed unthinkingly into parenthood, by intention or otherwise, only to be shocked by the heavy burden they have brought upon themselves? With children, the arc of care expands dramatically, and with it the possibility of grief. Anxiety for the other is now part of everyday life. One's freedom is also drastically curtailed. Only an absurdly sentimentalized view of parenthood could deny these evident truths. And, again, it is a regrettable fact that many parents do literally flee in the face of the burden. All must flee—or at least recoil—inwardly, at least to the extent of sensing the awesome responsibility they have assumed. Looked at from the child's point of view, this burdensomeness cannot help but shape one's feelings about oneself, and will only fuel the resentment that comes from sheer independent existence. To be thrust into the world of hunger and fear and death and *then* to be treated as a burden by the perpetrators—that must seem the very height of injustice. The child feels that she is *owed* her parents' full attention, while the parents jib at the weight they have taken on. Hard though it may be to accept, there is an undeniable conflict of interest between parent and child, considered purely prudentially. In the case of Victor and his 'child' the conflict reaches epic proportions. Later, the Creature will severely berate his 'father' for failing to carry out his parental duties: Victor buckled under the burden of fatherhood. How many other children have done the same to their fathers?

Next, the Creature, abandoned by Victor, wanders the countryside alone and shunned. He has been cast loose into the wide, windy world. When they finally meet up again, he says to Victor: 'Before I had quitted your apartment, on a sensation of cold, I had covered myself with some clothes; but these were insufficient to secure me from the dews of night. I was a poor, helpless, miserable wretch; I knew and could distinguish nothing; but feeling pain invade me on all sides, I sat down and wept' (99). Plainly, he is here appealing to the compassion of he who made him: he needed protection from the cruel lashes of Nature. This is obviously an experience with which we can easily identify; it could be *us* out there in the wet and cold. The Creature's early life is indeed recounted with the clear intention of recapitulating the normal development of humans, both ontogenetic and phylogenetic. Sometimes he resembles a babe in the woods; at others he is primeval man retreading the history of the race. His experiences mirror ours. Indistinct sensations gradually give way to clear perceptions; fire is discovered and prized; the barbarity of man and nature become evident. Maturity grows in him much as it does in us.

His first encounters with humans are hostile, being governed solely by his repulsive appearance. By no means are his own intentions violent at this stage: he is gentle and kind, despite the fearsome visage. He naturally feels the injustice of his rejection. He is also continuously subject to the ravages of nature—of cold and hunger, discomfort and fear. It is a hard, perilous world into which he has been involuntarily pitched. These too are human universals. We are judged by our physical appearance, our clothes, our origins. We may be irrationally rejected simply because we are physically different from others (racism is the most obvious analogy here, but clearly there are many forms of bodily prejudice). We may inspire fear in others despite our benign intentions and worthy actions. The bodily exterior is simply easier to observe than the inner self, and tends to dominate in social interactions, with untoward results. The eye is a superficial organ. The felt split between inner and outer is sharpened by these social reactions—the sense of one's body as an unreliable emissary. There is the feeling that we need constantly to transcend our outward appearance, to induce others to see us 'as we really are'. The Creature's early experiences in the big world resemble our own in the school playground, where we first become aware that we *have* a physical appearance and that it largely—and unfairly—controls how we are treated.

Then, too, we are all subject to the rigours of nature—cold, damp, wind, fire, the threat of death. The Creature, it is true, has no home to shelter and support him, while we (usually) do, but he makes us see the fragility of our own arrangements for subduing hostile nature. We might all too easily become homeless and hungry, exposed to the elements, our nights spent under the frosty stars. Nature might destroy our home, by flood or fire or earthquake, leaving us prey to uncaring forces. Distressingly little stands between our normal protections and the brutalities of nature. We are closer to the Creature than we care to recognize. The fear of being rejected, homeless, and alone is part of general human anxiety. Indeed, in a deep sense, we are already all three: we are rejected by at least some of those whom we want to accept us, and we are seldom accepted enough by those who do not reject us; our technology does not afford us a final protection against nature; and we are all separate, autonomous, solitary selves, from birth to death. It is a matter of degree, of detail, but the basic condition of the Creature is the human condition: social and natural vulnerability. We are all creatures of mere flesh and blood in a world not noted for its softness; fragile monsters to a man.

A particularly poignant phase of the Creature's life involves a family he observes through a chink in the wall of the hovel in which he has taken up residence. They have been cheated and dispossessed, despite their manifest virtue. They are unaware of the Creature's presence as he watches them go about their family business. He regards them as his friends, especially the blind father, bringing wood for them during the night—to their happy bafflement. He learns to speak and read by observing them, and becomes generally civilized.

I found that these people possessed a means of communicating their experience and feelings to one another by articulate sounds. I perceived that the words they spoke sometimes produced pleasure or pain, smiles or sadness, in the minds and countenances of the hearers. This was indeed a godlike science, and I ardently desired to become acquainted with it . . . By great application . . . I discovered the names that were given to some of the most familiar objects of discourse; I learned and applied the words 'fire', 'milk', 'bread', and 'wood'. (108–9)

This could be St Augustine discoursing on how he acquired language,[6] and doubtless Mary Shelley was familiar with the

---

[6] See section 1 of Wittgenstein's *Philosophical Investigations*, in which Augustine is quoted.

contemporary theories concerning language acquisition and mental development. Through acquiring language the Creature becomes truly one of us; he acquires the capacity that defines the human community. Now he can *talk* to us. He is no longer a speechless alien, grunting and howling. He has *reason*.

The identification with the ordinary human condition is reinforced by the arrival of Safie, an Arabian girl who also cannot speak the local language and who has also been grievously wronged. The Creature even boasts of his linguistic superiority to Safie: 'My days were spent in close attention, that I might more speedily master the language and I may boast that I improved more rapidly than the Arabian, who understood very little, and conversed in broken accents, whilst I comprehended and could imitate almost every word that was spoken' (115). It was, after all, his first language, his mother tongue, while Safie was struggling to learn her second. Here, clearly, it is the closeness of the Creature to us that is being stressed, not the distance. Later, when he learns of the organization of society and the course of history, he compares himself to the slave and vagabond, saying: 'I knew that I possessed no money, no friends, no kind of property' (116). He is the underdog, the downtrodden, the dispossessed. He is you in your worst nightmare.

At this stage of his life his character is still virtuous and mild, despite his earlier rejections. 'As yet I looked upon crime as a distant evil; benevolence and generosity were ever present before me, inciting within me a desire to become an actor in the busy scene where so many admirable qualities were called forth and displayed' (124). He could, at this point, be any hopeful adolescent, bent on achievement and virtue: who knows, perhaps he will become a great writer or politician or . . . ? He pointedly asks, 'Who was I? What was I? Whence did I come? What was my destination?' (125)—just as any reflective adolescent might. He feels his mental powers grow inside him and wonders what he will make of them.

He also compares himself to Adam, aptly enough—for Adam, too, was fatherless in the conventional sense. Reading Milton's *Paradise Lost*, he remarks: 'I often referred the several situations, as their similarity struck me, to my own. Like Adam, I was apparently united by no link to any other being in existence' (126). He is really an unblinkered Adam, searingly hypersensitive to his contingency and bodily constitution—'an imperfect and solitary being' (107) cast into the world. Both also experience a fall from innocence to evil; though the Creature's fall is mediated largely by aesthetic considerations—his ugliness—while Adam's stems from epistemological ones—he comes to know too much. It is Victor's fate that originates in a thirst for godlike knowledge, with the scientist playing the role of God. The difference between the Creature and Adam, as the Creature sees it, is that God paid more attention to the beauty of his creation: 'God, in pity, made man beautiful and alluring, after his own image, but my form is a filthy type of yours, more horrid even from the very resemblance. Satan had his companions, fellow-devils, to admire and encourage him, but I am solitary and abhorred' (127). But, as we have seen, this is to exaggerate the aesthetic excellence of man (are our *insides* also made in the image of God?), as well as our social felicity. We are *all* grotesquely formed and socially isolated, considered more deeply.

When the Creature chooses to reveal himself to the cottagers his reception is hostile and uncomprehending, despite some earlier success with the blind father. The monstrous intruder is beaten by the son, the sister faints, and the Creature flees the scene. Instead of the friendship and sympathy he has craved, he is treated as a dangerous enemy. As he justly remarks: 'My life has been hitherto harmless and in some degree beneficial, but a fatal prejudice clouds their eyes, and where they ought to see a feeling and kind friend, they behold only a detestable monster' (130). Understandably, this comes as a great blow to him and he resolves to visit terrible revenge on his creator for consigning him to such a miserable existence. He begins life innocently enough, is judged by morally irrelevant criteria, is unjustly rejected and punished, and only then begins to feel the urge for revenge. It is the sense of extreme injustice that fuels his eventual rage. This injustice has its origin in the dominance of *sight* in human relations: it is the way the Creature *looks* that fixes his fate. If everyone were blind, then he could hope for a fairer reception, but so powerful is the sense of sight that it obliterates every other consideration. His life is ruined by the contingent fact that people have eyes and an aesthetic sense.[7] In a way, it is just his bad luck that things are

[7] I once had an idea for a short story (never executed) to illustrate this point

arranged thus. Here we see a mirror held up for all the contingencies that determine the fate of human beings. We all carry this crushing weight of luck around with us, determining our destiny, and which strikes us as strictly extrinsic to what we essentially are. It all seems so radically *accidental*. Had the Creature been created beautiful, instead of ugly, no doubt things would have gone very differently for him. He is the victim of his own contingent shell; as we too are the victims of the shell of contingencies that surrounds our existence.

The episode with the cottagers can easily be read as a parable of human friendship, at least in some of its manifestations. Extreme attachments are formed, with high expectations of felicity, without real knowledge of the potential friends in anything but a superficial way. One espies them from afar, through a chink, so to speak—though one may see and converse with them every day. They seem to answer to some ideal of human companionship. One tries to move nearer, in some trepidation, hoping to create that special bond of intimacy. One is painfully aware that they have only one's outer identity to go on. One wants to overcome isolation, the sense of watching others from the wings, perhaps envying them their happy, smooth relationships. But they may refuse one's gesture of friendship, possibly because of some irrelevant and insignificant fact. One may be feared for no good reason. And even if one does engage in a friendship, there is always the danger of rejection and misunderstanding. A doubt is always present: do they care enough? How loyal are they? When would they betray? Human relationships are only too full of such questions and anxieties. The concept of *trust* is deeply woven into all our social dealings, and it is a concept with enormous emotional potential, for good or ill. The Creature tried to trust his cottagers and paid mightily for it in emotional damage. His friends betrayed him. From now on he is governed more by hatred than by anything else.

---

about sight. The basic mechanism of the plot was to be the acquisition of sight by a community or race who have hitherto been totally blind. What would happen to the existing marriages when the partners come to see what their spouses look like?

4. RAGE, REVENGE, ENVY

There is nothing incomprehensible about the sea change in the Creature's psychology: he reacts with understandable anger towards those who have treated him unjustly. Soon after the incident with the cottagers, he receives yet another violent rebuff: he is cruelly shot by a peasant after saving a drowning girl's life, again because of his fearsome appearance. He reports the upshot: 'The mildness of my nature had fled, and all within me was turned to gall and bitterness' (135). He now becomes violent, *inwardly* monstrous, seeking the destruction of everything that is dear to his neglectful creator. He first murders Victor's young brother; then he frames the innocent Justine for the murder and revels in her execution; he murders Victor's best friend, Clerval; finally he strangles Victor's bride, the lovely Elizabeth, on her wedding night. His vengeance is certainly extreme, but he is presented as having a just complaint—that Victor created him only to leave him to a wretched and lonely existence. *He*, at least, should have stuck by his progeny and tolerated his physical imperfections. The Creature's well-meaning actions and kindly feelings have been rebuffed and trampled upon; he has been made the victim of great injustices, and now he must have his revenge. The envy he feels for Victor's contented normal life—his family, his friends, his bride—pushes him towards his evil acts. His thirst for revenge is thus humanly intelligible.

We may not commit the kinds of crimes the Creature does, but the feelings that prompt him are not alien to us. We too can suffer the sting of rejection based merely upon appearance; we can be envious of those who do not suffer (as we think) our social exclusion. It can seem that other people lead a charmed life from which we are unfairly excluded. Victor's social life of family and friends is no doubt preposterously idealized—no one enjoys such pure felicity in human relationships. But this is still how we are prone to imagine the lives of those fortunate others (until the curtain is rudely pulled back). Our own life tends to feel impoverished in relation to this ideal. And even if we feel quite lucky in our personal relationships, we still carry a picture in our heads that transcends what can be achieved in mortal life. We have the idea of a social utopia compared to which our actual life is sadly imperfect. So we can readily understand the Creature's sentiments: his rage is intelligible to us, because it is a rage we are acquainted with in attenuated form. When he explains to Victor what his life has been like, we see that his life could have been ours. We even see that it *is* ours, viewed in an oblique and magnified way.

The Creature offers Victor a way out of the vengeance he has planned for him. This is to create for him a female mate, also assembled from dead bodies, also ugly and spurned by humanity. Victor comes close to fulfilling this request, in order that he shall be left alone by his 'son'. But he backs down at the last minute— fearing what the pair of them might visit upon humanity, concerned that the female will also reject the male, worried that she *won't* reject him and terrible offspring will be unleashed upon the earth. So the Creature is denied even this balm to his isolation, despite his vow to depart to the frozen north with his mate and never trouble humanity again. Here again, the Creature's psychology is familiar to us. We too seek the soothing partner who will be sufficient society for us, who will accept our imperfections, who will not reject us as others have. We seek a kind of ideal bonding in romantic love, an ultimate solution to the problem of loneliness. *That*, we feel, would fulfil our most fundamental needs. But, like the Creature, we fail to find what we seek. Nothing seems to add up to what we hoped for. The self remains essentially unbreached, moated and walled in on all sides.[8] Human desire has a kind of necessary unfulfillability built into it: it is hyperbolic, unrealistic, implacably platonic. What we imagine is always purer and finer than what we achieve. This is why the satisfaction of desire, especially romantic desire, often brings the greatest depression and disillusionment. Imagination infuses desire, and imagination takes us to impossible worlds of fulfilment and bliss.[9] Thus, we know what it means to have our hopes of romantic bliss snatched away from us. Victor actually tears up the Creature's future mate before his very eyes—an exceptionally

[8] Imagery like this abounds in the writings of Bertrand Russell, who seems to have felt his isolation from others with searing acuity. See the biography by Ray Monk, *Bertrand Russell: the Spirit of Solitude.*

[9] Contrast animal desire, which *can* be satisfied. Animals have desires without the imagination of ideals—or so it seems. The satisfaction conditions of their desires are hence realistically this-worldly. An animal does not—sensibly enough— yearn for the inherently unattainable.

vivid and horrific way to see one's romantic hopes shattered. The Creature is disappointed in love even before his bride takes her first breath.

The Creature is, in sum, a being who lives these bleak truths of human life concretely and practically: he dramatizes the essential structure of our existence; his life makes a philosophical point about who and what we are.

5. 'I WILL BE WITH YOU ON YOUR WEDDING-NIGHT'

If the Creature is not to be granted a mate of his own, then he will see to it that Victor does not enjoy conjugal bliss either. He warns Victor of this: 'Man! you may hate, but beware! your hours will pass in dread and misery, and soon the bolt will fall which must ravish from you your happiness forever. Are you to be happy, while I grovel in the intensity of my wretchedness?' (162). He then issues his dread threat: '*I will be with you on your wedding-night.*' This phrase is then repeated in the text several times, always in italics, and most pointedly. It does not itself *say* that any murder will be committed, though that is what happens. The phrase itself is enigmatically sinister and suggestive. What is its meaning? Why is it produced with such vehemence? It has a curious ring to it, offering itself as a riddle of some sort. A hint of collaboration or collusion appears to be intended. But of what kind? It is certainly tragically misunderstood by Victor, who takes it as veiled threat to murder him; while the astute reader guesses that the Creature's target is rather to be his bride, Elizabeth. Here Victor seems to be almost wilfully avoiding what should have been perfectly obvious—the outcome of his error being the murder of his bride.

One might think to detect a note of the homoerotic in the phrase: the Creature is saying that *he* will be with Victor, conjugally speaking, not Elizabeth. But this has no echo in other aspects of the story, and the Creature's sexuality is clearly on the heterosexual side. It is not, then, that he intends to take the place of the bride on the night. I want to suggest, in line with the general interpretation I am proposing, that the Creature's meaning, disguised as it is, is as follows: that on his wedding-night, Victor will *himself* be a monster. The monster will be 'with' him in the sense that he will then have a monstrous identity. I do not know if Mary Shelley consciously intended this meaning,[10] but it does make sense of what is otherwise a literary puzzle, and it fits the overall theme of the book, as I am interpreting it. The thought is that on Victor's wedding-night, which is also the night of Elizabeth's sexual initiation, an act of some bestiality will be performed, an act involving violation and blood. From being the loving and gentle brother-figure, Victor will be transformed into a sexual monster. Not only does sex reveal the more monstrous side of the human body; it also reveals a monstrous psychology. It requires an act of monstrous violation, accompanied by monstrous frenzy. So, at any rate, it might seem to a young virgin at the beginning of the nineteenth century. The bride's apprehensions take the form of a fear of the monster that will emerge from her new husband on the night of her defloration. *She* will be with a monster on her wedding-night.

The Creature clearly declares that he will be there on the night of sexual initiation; and that he will be *with* Victor, as if in collaboration. Now what actually happens on that night? Foolishly leaving Elizabeth alone, Victor paces the hallways in search of the Creature. Then:

I heard a shrill and dreadful scream. It came from the room into which Elizabeth had retired . . . She was there, lifeless and inanimate, thrown across the bed, her head hanging down, and her pale and distorted features half covered by her hair. Every where I turn I see the same figure— her bloodless arms and relaxed form flung by the murderer on its bridal bier. (189)

That she has been ravished and raped by the Creature is not out of the question; she has certainly been physically violated by him on her bridal bed. The Creature has perpetrated a violent act on her that might be thought to symbolize the sexual act Victor was about to perform; an exaggerated fear of first sexual intercourse might well conceive it in such hyperbolic terms. The Creature has indeed been a violent monster to Elizabeth on her wedding-

---

[10] My suspicion, however, is that she did, but she thought it politic to keep the suggestion distinctly *sotto voce*. The phrase is repeated with such archness that some such subtext must be lurking in the background.

night, as Victor might have been a monster of a lesser stripe. The analogy between them is certainly there to be found.

The reason, then, that the Creature's ominous phrase is so highlighted is to draw attention to the monstrous nature of male sexual design. The suggestion is that sex can make a man into another kind of being, driven and violent, unrecognizable, bestial. The Creature, after all, is a *male* monster, equipped with all the desires and appendages that characterize that peculiar sub-variety of the type. Obviously, this suggestion is not overtly stated in the text—it would be indelicate, to put it mildly, to do so—but it is not implausible to detect its presence there. The sexual monster is, after all, one of the more accessible manifestations of monster-hood.

6. DEATH

And how does the Creature die? Alone and at the mercy of the fiercer elements, fire and ice—burning on a raft in an arctic ocean. His death is dramatic and primordial. He dies without ever relieving for a moment the torment of his isolation. Once Victor is dead he no longer has a reason to live, since every human contact he has ever had has now been extinguished. 'I shall die. I shall no longer feel the agonies which now consume me, or be the prey of feelings unsatisfied, yet unquenched. He is dead who called me into being; and when I shall be no more, the very remembrance of us both will speedily vanish' (214). Death, for him, is the only solution to the agony of isolation. He dies alone, and because he is alone.

But this aloneness again has its counterpart in human experience. We are never more alone than in death, as the individual consciousness takes its solitary journey into non-existence (or wherever). No one can accompany us, hold our hand; in dying we move outside the sphere of human contact. And just as the only ultimate solution to the Creature's loneliness is death, so it is with us: the solipsistic predicament is ended only when the self is no longer around to feel its essential separation from others. I stop being *not* you only when I no longer *am*. Since it is the essential nature of the self to be alone, this condition can only be ended by the cessation of the self.

The Creature dies by fire. Fire is perhaps the most dramatic and terrifying of the elemental forces—ravenous and blind, ethereal yet deadly. Fire represents the anarchic and uncontrollable in nature, and we fear it more than anything else. Mere flesh has no hope against its feathery touch. Fire can sustain life, but it can as easily take it away. Death by fire is nature asserting its utter power over human existence. But in this respect fire symbolizes all the unstoppable forces that lead to our extinction. We are all consumed by such natural enemies in the end. The Creature has battled nature all his life, but he finally succumbs to it. And that is what we all must do, sooner or later. Nature is the inescapable agent of death: it is the ultimate destructive monster.

7. CONCLUSION

I have suggested that the Creature's life is a model or mirror of human life; not in the trite sense that 'we all have an evil side', but in the sense that his very being represents the essential structure of human existence. My point, of course, is not that this bleak picture of human life is the whole truth; but it is part of the truth—the part we prefer to ignore. In *Frankenstein*, we are enabled to live this part of the truth imaginatively, by projecting it onto a being we can think of as alien to us. Yet all the while we are projecting it outwards we are exploring our own fears and uncertainties. The Creature fascinates us because we see so much of ourselves in him in disguised form. It feels safe to explore our own condition in this way because we can tell ourselves that it is all happening to someone else. To treat this material directly, putting the reader consciously into the position he or she is really in anyway, would be too troubling; so it is done obliquely and metaphorically. The story seems especially popular with young people, particularly adolescents, and I conjecture that this is because the dark truths about human life that it contains are dawning in the minds of the young. Their peeled eyes and undulled minds are ready to receive these harsh realities. As I have remarked, Mary Shelley was herself scarcely out of adolescence when she composed the story. The perils of the natural world, the problematic nature of the family, the difficulties of human society, the realities of the body and its social role, the prospect of life-long entrapment in one's own subjectivity, envy of others, feelings of injustice, rage, extremes of elation and despair—all these bear down on the adolescent consciousness in full force. After a while we tend to become numbed to these elemental facts, or to evolve ways of protecting ourselves from them; but the adolescent eye is apt to be beady and dilated and self-conscious.

There is a certain consoling message in all this bleakness, however. If the sentimentalized family life of Victor is really just a sham, then at least we are all in the same basic predicament: we are all Frankenstein's monster and none of us is Frankenstein. In the end the Creature reduces Victor's condition to something close to his own, thus asserting the unreality of the earlier depiction of Victor's life. The Creature has forced the truth onto the world by brutely physical means. His wretched condition becomes the norm. He annihilates the distance between himself and us. We are each of us living in the same private hell. We are all solitary monsters, careering through the wilderness, full of bitterness and regret, waiting for death to relieve our isolation. It is not that some of us lead ontologically charmed lives, while others are condemned to monstrosity; we are *all* grotesque vehicles of ineliminable solitude. If I were Victor, I would have urged this point of view on the Creature: then he would have seen that his condition was not quite as unique as he supposed. There was, in a way, really no need for him to revenge himself on Victor by bringing their lives closer together, since they *already* existed in the same essential predicament—as we all do. At a mundane and superficial level, of course, there are vast differences between Victor and his creation; but there exists a perspective from which they do not differ *toto caelo*.

And there is one more point that the story illustrates: how quotidian truths can be given interest and form by being expressed in an imaginative narrative. There are certain fundamental facts that need constantly to be rediscoverd and reformulated, because of their importance to us; but to state them in plain form, as I have above, is often to strip them of vitality and reduce them to banalities. But banalities are often what we most need to exercise our minds around, without their appearing to us as banalities. An effective work of fiction is precisely a refashioning of the obvious in such a way that we are enabled to experience it afresh. There is no need to say anything new, just to remind the reader of what he or she already knows, if only implicitly. That is what *Frankenstein* succeeds so impressively in doing: Mary Shelley found a way of stating the obvious while appearing to tell of extraordinary events. As Percy Bysshe Shelley astutely remarks in the Preface to *Frankenstein*, the book 'affords a point of view to the imagination for the delineating of human passions more comprehensive and commanding than any which the ordinary relations of existing events can yield' (11). Thus the extraordinariness of the ordinary is brought home to us.

8

Conclusion: Stories and Morals

Recent moral philosophy in the analytical tradition has paid a good deal of attention to language. It asks such questions as: are moral utterances factual statements or are they expressions of emotion or disguised imperatives? Is there any kind of 'is' from which an 'ought' can be derived? How are words like 'brave' and 'generous' to be analysed? What does it mean to say that someone has a right? What is the referent of 'good'? Yet despite this focus on moral language it has seldom been asked which mode of discourse is most appropriate for conveying ethical information or evoking ethical reflection. How do we use language to make moral points? What kinds of 'text' are deemed suitable for moral instruction? Here we need to look at the larger structures of moral discourse, in which moral claims are made persuasive. The unit of persuasive discourse in science is the *theory*—what then is the unit of moral persuasion? How in fact do we convey and derive moral lessons? By not asking this question, analytical moral philosophy has, I think, narrowed the study of ethics rather unnaturally, not only at the linguistic level but also in terms of the topics that are discussed. In conclusion, then, I want to look briefly and programmatically at the relation between morals and types of text (where 'text' includes any kind of linguistic performance, spoken or written, or even just thought about).

There are, I suggest, two traditional paradigms of what a moral text should look like, both handily exemplified in the Bible. One type of text is typified by the Ten Commandments: a list of moral directives, in this case dictated by God, designed to be memorized and obeyed—'Thou shalt not steal', etc. The sentence forms here are simple and unqualified, and the injunctions they contain are meant to be followed mechanically. The list composes something like a moral manual—what to do in order to be a good person. There is no attempt to relate the moral directives to character or motivation or concrete context; the ethical prescriptions exist in their own independent realm, expressing the divine will or the moral law. They resemble the axioms of Euclidean geometry in their abstractness and universality. (Spinoza, famously, attempted to compose a moral text modelled upon Euclid's *Elements*.)[1] And they have all the merits of clarity, force, and memorability. Inscribe them on your heart, and you will not go far wrong. Call this the *commandment* style of moral discourse.

But there is another style of imparting moral lessons, much favoured by Jesus of Nazareth as a method of ethical education: the parable. Here a narrative is constructed in which concrete characters take part, equipped with intelligible motivations and personalities, confronted by situations of choice—as, say, with the parable of the Prodigal Son.[2] Metaphor may be extensively employed (as, notably, with the parable of the Sower),[3] and the parable often takes the form of a riddle in asking for some work of interpretation on the listener's part. It typically terminates with a question which tests the listener's grasp of the moral issues raised (consider the parable of the Talents).[4] This type of moral text operates by engaging the listener's mastery of folk psychology and applying it in a dramatic or narrative context; the ethical lesson is meant to fall out of this activation of co-operating faculties. It is precisely *not* like Euclid's *Elements* or any other scientific treatise. Rather, the parable is a small work of art that invites aesthetic evaluation as well as moral attention. It exploits the power of the story form in order to teach a moral lesson. Accordingly, it needs to be *interpreted*, not merely memorized word for word. The material must be mentally processed and digested. Call this the *parable* style of moral discourse.

My impression is that philosophers have been too influenced by the commandment paradigm and not enough by the parable paradigm. Moral discourse has been construed as essentially a list of moral directives or affirmations, and the only question is the proper analysis of these directives or affirmations. 'Stealing is wrong': what is the correct analysis of that sentence? This ten-

---

[1] Benedictus de Spinoza, *Ethics, Demonstrated in Geometrical Order.*
[2] Luke 15.   [3] Matthew 13.   [4] Luke 19.

dency probably reflects the cultural tradition in which philosophers stand, at least in terms of how moral issues are set up. Moral education has been mainly conducted by means of sentences of the form 'Do this, don't do that!' But the tendency is also reinforced by the influence of science: an ethical *system* or *theory* must be devised, consisting of laws and axioms, analogous to the principles of physics and chemistry. The Ten Commandments have the same basic structure as Newton's laws or the Periodic table: a list of isolable units, universal in logical form, which together govern the way things ought to be. These moral laws (note the word) tend to concern actions and the word 'ought' figures prominently in their formulation. Moral thinking is concerned fundamentally with what we *ought to do*. This conception is also abetted by a view of morality as analogous to a set of laws in the legal sense—a list of statutes permitting and prohibiting various actions, with penalties attaching. Imperceptibly, ethics comes to be the study of ethical rules of action—normative generalizations about how one should conduct oneself. Such rules can be readily preached from the pulpit; they can also be learned by rote in the way so much mathematics and science tends to be. And they call for little in the way of subtlety or interpretation: the recipient is encouraged passively to absorb the moral prescriptions in question, and then to act on them. Such prescriptions are also convenient items for tidy-minded moral philosophers to fasten upon—islands of relative clarity in what can seem a confusing and messy moral life. Techniques of logical analysis can be smoothly applied, with results announced and QEDs appended. You know where you are with a commandment.

But alongside this tradition of ethical expression, and in many ways in competition with it, we have the story form, which includes not just the parable but also the play and the short story and the narrative poem and the novel and the film. In these forms ethical themes are dramatically enacted, characters displayed, comedy and tragedy brought to bear. Art is used to serve morality, and in many different ways.[5] Here it is not our scientific

---

[5] I am not, of course, saying that this is *all* that literary art does—just that it is an important part of it. In fact, I think that the role of morality in fiction has been underestimated in recent years, mainly because of the relativism and formalism

faculties and modes of thought that are activated, but our artistic faculties, in all their complexity and ramifications. We must draw upon an enormous background of tacit knowledge about human life, not clearly codifiable into theoretical principles, and our aesthetic responses are centrally implicated. This takes us into new territory, in which the scientifically trained analytical philosopher is apt to feel professionally uncomfortable. Yet ordinary people —which means all of us—find this mode of moral discourse uniquely palatable and nutritious; it seems perfectly designed to engage our moral faculties. Our moral understanding and the story form seem fitted for one another. No rote learning is necessary: it all seems to flow quite naturally. This is the way our moral faculty *likes* to operate. It is almost effortless to take in a story, pleasant even, though the story may be replete with moral significance.

The novel, in particular, is a text of a very different kind from the scientific treatise. It is also very different from the philosophical text, which is what philosophers, naturally, are most comfortable with. Thus the novel form has tended to be ignored by moral philosophers: it is not, for them, the place to look for canonical expressions of ethical truth.[6] Yet, quite obviously, it is for most educated people one of the prime vehicles of ethical exploration. (Film plays a similar role for the less word-minded.) In reading a novel we have ethical experiences, sometimes quite profound ones, and we reach ethical conclusions, condemning some characters and admiring others. We *live* a particular set of moral challenges (sitting there in our armchair) by entering into the lives of the characters introduced. Often the novel serves to crystallize some common human experience, giving it imaginative spin—as I argued in the case of *Frankenstein* in the previous chapter. Stories can sharpen and clarify moral questions, encouraging a dialectic between the reader's own experience and the trials of the characters he or she is reading about. A tremendous amount of moral thinking and feeling is done when reading novels (or

that afflict so much of contemporary literary studies. I would say that it is simply not possible to discuss literature adequately without seriously taking on the ethical dimensions of the text.

   [6] An exception is Nussbaum, *Love's Knowledge*. See also Rorty, *Contingency, Irony, and Solidarity*, Part III. This commonality of concern should not, however, disguise the deep differences in our respective approaches.

watching plays and films, or reading poetry and short stories). In fact, it is not an exaggeration to say that for most people this is the primary way in which they acquire ethical attitudes, especially in contemporary culture. Our ethical knowledge is aesthetically mediated. There is a clear interplay between art and ethics in moral education: the artistic and the ethical are processed simultaneously and in complex interpenetrating ways. This is not the simple commandment approach to ethics, but it is an approach that works and which is enormously prevalent. I take this to be so obvious that I am almost embarrassed to state it.

For all this, however, moral philosophers systematically ignore the role of fictional works in ethical understanding. One of my aims in this book has been to rectify this tendency. Some attempt should be made to come to terms with the embeddedness of the ethical in the fictional. For this we need new methods and styles with which to discuss stories and morals. Our discussions will be less abstract and more immediate, since we are now closer to lived ethical experience. The ethical will be seen to be inextricably bound up with other concerns, particularly aesthetic ones, but also with specific details of character and context. The universally quantified ethical prescription will not be the standard form here (not that I object to that form in its proper place). We will need to mingle the general and the specific in ways that are not typical of the orthodox ethical treatise. Above all, questions of *character* assume far greater prominence when ethics is approached in this way, since fictional works are all about the interaction between character and conduct. The orthodox focus on moral norms and types of action will be an inadequate tool. To evaluate someone ethically you need to be able to analyse his or her character, and fiction still provides the best conceptual equipment for doing that (and probably always will). In fiction, character is the *sine qua non*. Character is to fiction what space and time are to physics.

This opens up a whole region of moral interest that is not covered by the usual division into metaethics and normative ethics. This book has attempted to occupy some of that region, showing its potential fertility. It is not that these questions *cannot* in principle be pursued except by placing them in a literary context; but they are most naturally investigated in that context, and they are often fruitfully suggested by works of fiction. It helps enormously to have a particular character in a specific context with whom to raise and test ethical ideas. Without this specificity the discussion is apt to become lifeless and unmoored, the moral generalities hanging limply in the air. The strength of an ethical idea lies in its applications, in how it *plays out*. In fiction, we can put an ethical idea through its paces, testing its ability to command our assent. We can also explore its alignments, limitations, repercussions. We can face moral reality in all its complexity and drama.

The fictional work can make us *see* and *feel* good and evil in a way that no philosophical tract can—unless it takes on board what literary works achieve so well. The deadness and vapidity often alleged against academic moral philosophy would not be felt if it took more seriously the role of fiction in moral discourse. For moral experience lives by the story. I often notice how much more engaged and perceptive my students are when I teach ethics from literature rather than from a philosophical text. Nor do I detect much of the usual (depressing) sophomoric relativism in their moral comments when their minds are focused on the deeds of particular characters. I take this as evidence that the literary works are recruiting their real moral faculties: they are down in the moral trenches, outraged or compassionate, fully immersed in moral concepts, not distracted by philosophical irrelevancies.[7]

It might be objected that my insistence on the narrative form as a vehicle of moral thought is quite consistent with favouring episodes from real life as our focus of interest. Why not turn our attention to biography, history, news reports? For these are all concrete narrative forms concerning specific individuals—they are simply not fictional. I have no deep objection of principle to this suggestion; indeed, I think the optimum procedure is a kind of interplay between the factual and the fictional. But there are good reasons why, in practice, fact does not work anything like as well as fiction. This is simply because the techniques of *art* are

---

[7] Scepticism about morality seems hollow when the moral faculties are practically engaged—just as scepticism about the external world is the furthest thing from one's mind in the heat of battle. The doubts in both cases are *philosophical* doubts, not 'real' doubts (as Wittgenstein would say). It is remarkable how committed people become to morality when they are confronted by a real moral issue, even if only in fictional form; scepticism intrudes only when the engine is idling.

missing from straight factual discourse. The narrative artist structures her story according to aesthetic criteria, and she fashions her characters and the events in which they participate with specific themes in mind. Thus all the benefits of artistic structure accrue to the moral material that is being enacted—coherence, transparency, aesthetic form, creative talent. The artist *constructs* her story with certain aims in mind, partly or largely moral; she makes her characters available to the reader so that they can be appreciated in their essence.[8] We do not have the problem of opacity that afflicts our access to people and events in real life— the problem of what really happened, of what someone's motivation really was. The novelist can simply tell the reader what is true of her characters; she can just hand you the information you need in order to ground your moral assessments. There is also the advantage that no real person's fate turns upon what you judge, so that you feel freer to explore and condemn what is presented. The fictional world is really the ideal world in which to go on ethical expeditions: it is safe, convenient, inconsequential, and expressly designed for our exploration and delight. Logan Pearsall Smith famously remarked, 'People say that life is the thing, but I prefer reading.'[9] That is no doubt a shade too bookish for most of us, but it has a lot to recommend it as a way of acquiring ethical knowledge.

Let me end by mentioning a commonplace, but one that should have more impact on philosophical thinking about morals than it does. It is often reported that reading a certain novel 'changed my life', and there is no doubt of the transformative power of the novel over the reader. (James Joyce's *Portrait of the Artist as a Young Man* made a big impact on me at the age of eighteen.) And such profound revisions of outlook are typically ethical in character. A novel can instil an entirely new ethical perspective in the reader. It is as if we ourselves live through the events of the story and are thereby influenced to come to a new moral vision. (The mysteriousness of this process is part of its power.) The novel acts as moral spur and guide, bringing moral

---

[8] The novels of Jane Austen are perhaps the most obvious illustration of this point: they are lucid essays—or tests—in character evaluation, plain and simple (though not unsophisticated, by any means).

[9] Logan Pearsall Smith, *Afterthoughts* (1931), 'Myself'.

upheavals of varying magnitudes. Isn't this something that philosophers of morality should pay more attention to? Doesn't it demonstrate the ethical importance of the story form? I think myself that this kind of imaginative experience is one of the main engines of moral life. The story of morals is the story of moral stories.

BIBLIOGRAPHY

Amis, Kingsley. *Lucky Jim* (New York: Penguin, 1954).

Aristotle. *Ethics* (Harmondsworth: Penguin, 1976).

Ayer, A. J. *Language, Truth and Logic* (New York: Dover, 1952).

Benacerraf, Paul. 'Mathematical Truth', in Paul Benacerraf and Hilary Putnam (eds.), *Philosophy of Mathematics*, 2nd edn. (Cambridge: Cambridge University Press, 1983), pp. 403–20.

Buford, Bill. *Among the Thugs* (New York: Random House, 1993).

Chomsky, Noam. *Language and Problems of Knowledge: The Managua Lectures* (Cambridge, Mass.: MIT Press, 1988).

Dyer, Richard. *Brief Encounter* (London: BFI Publishing, 1993).

Harman, Gilbert. *The Nature of Morality* (New York: Oxford University Press, 1977).

Hume, David. *A Treatise of Human Nature*, 2nd edn., ed. L. A. Selby-Bigge (Oxford: Clarendon Press, 1978).

Husserl, Edmund. *Logical Investigations* (London: Routledge & Kegan Paul, 1970).

Kivy, Peter. 'Melville's *Billy* and the Secular Problem of Evil: The Worm in the Bud', *The Monist*, 63, no. 4 (October 1980), 480–93.

Kripke, Saul. *Wittgenstein on Rules and Private Language* (Cambridge, Mass.: Harvard University Press, 1982).

Kuhn, Thomas. *The Structure of Scientific Revolutions*, 2nd edn. (Chicago: University of Chicago Press, 1970).

Laclos, Choderlos de. *Les Liaisons Dangereuses* (New York: Oxford University Press, 1995).

Lewis, David, Johnston, Mark, and Smith, Michael. 'Dispositional Theories of Value', *Proceedings of the Aristotelian Society*, supp. vol. 65 (1989), 89–174.

Locke, John. *An Essay Concerning Human Understanding*, ed. Peter H. Nidditch (Oxford: Clarendon Press, 1975).

Mackie, J. L. *Ethics: Inventing Right and Wrong* (Harmondsworth: Penguin, 1977).

McDowell, John. 'Values and Secondary Qualities', in Geoffrey Sayre-McCord (ed.),*Essays on Moral Realism* (Ithaca, NY: Cornell University Press, 1988), 166–80.

McGinn, Colin. 'The Concept of Knowledge', in *Midwest Studies in Philosophy*, 9 (Minneapolis, Minn.: University of Minnesota Press, 1984), 529–54.
—— *The Subjective View* (Oxford: Clarendon Press, 1982).
—— *Mental Content* (Oxford: Basil Blackwell, 1989).
—— *Moral Literacy: Or, How to Do the Right Thing* (Indianapolis, Ind.: Hackett, 1991).
—— *The Problem of Consciousness* (Oxford: Basil Blackwell, 1991).
—— *Problems in Philosophy* (Oxford: Basil Blackwell, 1993).
Melville, Herman. *Billy Budd, Sailor and Other Stories* (New York: Bantam Books, 1981).
Miller, Robert, ed. *The Complete Gospels* (Sonoma, Calif.: Polebridge Press, 1994).
Monk, Ray. *Bertrand Russell: The Spirit of Solitude* (London: Jonathan Cape, 1996).
Moore, G. E. *Principia Ethica*, rev. edn. (Cambridge: Cambridge University Press, 1993).
—— 'The Conception of Intrinsic Value', in *Principia Ethica* , 280–98.
Nabokov, Vladimir. *Lolita*, ed. Alfred Appel, Jr. (New York: Vintage, 1991).
Nagel, Thomas. *What Does It All Mean? A Very Short Introduction to Philosophy* (New York: Oxford University Press, 1987).
Norton, Robert. *The Beautiful Soul: Aesthetic Morality in the Eighteenth Century* (Ithaca, NY: Cornell University Press, 1995.)
Nussbaum, Martha. *Love's Knowledge: Essays on Philosophy and Literature* (New York: Oxford University Press, 1990).
Perry, John. 'The Problem of the Essential Indexical', in Nathan Salmon and Scott Soames (eds.), *Propositions and Attitudes* (Oxford: Oxford University Press, 1988): 83-101.
Plato. *Republic*, in *Plato: Collected Dialogues*, ed. Edith Hamilton and Huntington Cairns (Princeton, NJ: Princeton University Press, 1961).
Rawls, John. *A Theory of Justice* (Cambridge, Mass.: Harvard University Press, 1971).
Reid, Thomas. *Essays on the Intellectual Powers of Man* (Cambridge, Mass.: MIT Press, 1969).
Rorty, Richard. *Contingency, Irony, and Solidarity* (Cambridge: Cambridge University Press, 1989).
Russell, Bertrand. *The Problems of Philosophy* (Oxford: Oxford University Press, 1912).
Sade, Marquis de. *The 120 Days of Sodom and Other Writings* (New York: Grove Press, 1966).
Sartre, Jean-Paul. *Being and Nothingness* (New York: Pocket Books, 1956).

Sayre-McCord, Geoffrey (ed.). *Essays on Moral Realism* (Ithaca, NY: Cornell University Press, 1988).

Shelley, Mary Wollestonecraft. *Frankenstein* (New York: Penguin, 1992).

Smith, Logan Pearsall. *All Trivia: Trivia, More Trivia, Afterthoughts, Last Words* (London: Constable, 1933).

Spinoza, Benedictus de. *Ethics* (New York: Hafner, 1949).

Tarski, Alfred. 'The Concept of Truth in Formalised Languages', in *Logic, Semantics, Metamathematics*, 2nd edn., ed. John Corcoran (Indianapolis, Ind.: Hackett, 1983), 152–278.

Watson, Lyall. *Dark Nature: A Natural History of Evil* (New York: HarperCollins, 1995).

Wilde, Oscar. *The Picture of Dorian Gray* (New York: Penguin, 1985).

Williams, Bernard. 'Internal and External Reasons', in *Moral Luck: Philosophical Papers, 1973–1980* (Cambridge: Cambridge University Press, 1981), 110–23.

—— *Ethics and the Limits of Philosophy* (London: Fontana, 1985).

Wittgenstein, Ludwig. *Philosophical Investigations* (New York: Macmillan, 1953).

INDEX